Finish Carpentry Basics

Created and Designed by the Editorial Staff of Ortho Books

Project Editor
Barbara Feller-Roth

Writers
Craig Bergquist
Charles Huddleston

Illustrators
Edith Allgood
Ron Hildebrand

Ortho Books

Publisher
Edward A. Evans

Editorial Director
Christine Jordan

Production Director
Ernie S. Tasaki

Managing Editors
Robert J. Beckstrom
Michael D. Smith
Sally W. Smith

System Manager
Linda M. Bouchard

Product Manager
Richard E. Pile, Jr.

Marketing Administrative Assistant
Daniel Stage

Distribution Specialist
Barbara F. Steadham

Operations Assistant
Georgiann Wright

Technical Consultant
J. A. Crozier, Jr., Ph.D.

No portion of this book may be reproduced without written permission from the publisher.

We are not responsible for unsolicited manuscripts, photographs, or illustrations.

Before purchasing materials discussed in this book, be sure to check with local building authorities to verify and review all construction steps.

Every effort has been made at the time of publication to guarantee the accuracy of the names and addresses of information sources and suppliers, and in the technical data and recommendations contained. However, readers should check for their own assurance and must be responsible for selection and use of suppliers, supplies, materials, and chemical products.

Address all inquiries to:
Ortho Books
Chevron Chemical Company
Consumer Products Division
Box 5047
San Ramon, CA 94583

Copyright © 1983, 1991
Chevron Chemical Company
All rights reserved under international and Pan-American copyright conventions.

1 2 3 4 5 6 7 8 9
91 92 93 94 95 96

ISBN 0-89721-236-3
Library of Congress Catalog Card Number 90-86163

Chevron Chemical Company
6001 Bollinger Canyon Road, San Ramon, CA 94583

Acknowledgments

Consultant
John Parr

Copy Chief
Melinda E. Levine

Editorial Coordinator
Cass Dempsey

Copyeditor
Irene Elmer

Proofreader
David Sweet

Indexer
Shirley J. Manley

Editorial Assistants
Deborah Bruner
Laurie A. Steele

Composition by
Nancy Patton Wilson-McCune

Layout by
Lezlly Freier

Production by
Studio 165

Separations by
Color Tech Corp.

Lithographed in the USA by
Webcrafters, Inc.

Special thanks to the following builders and cabinetmakers
San Francisco Restorations—Jim Mannix, Johnny Johnson, Michael Chromy, San Francisco, Calif.: front cover
Peter Blanco and Alfredo Thibeaux, San Francisco, Calif., builders: 62, 93
FAIR Group, San Francisco, Calif., developers: 62, 93
Bruce Imhoff, Athol, Mass., cabinetmaker and builder: 82

Thanks also to
Toolmaster Inc., Portola Hardware, and Carling Construction Co., San Francisco, Calif.
Waterstreet Company, Sausalito, Calif.
East of the Sun, Saugatuck, Mich.

Photographers
Names of photographers are followed by the page numbers on which their work appears.
R=right, C=center, L=left, T=top, B=bottom.

Michael Lamotte: 4
Fred Lyon: Title page, 3, 24, 33, 35, 39, 64, back cover
Kit Morris: Front cover, 22, 27, 42, 44, 62, 93
McKie Wing Roth, Jr.: 82
Dave Rowland, Courtesy Wood Moulding & Millwork Producers Association: 108, 109

Photographic Assistant
Mary Cancelmo

Front Cover
This handsome finish trim is made up of standard moldings available at any well-stocked building center. Such a column can be used for decorative purposes or to conceal utility lines or heating ducts.

Title Page
The workmanship and ingenuity that went into producing this tool chest are an inspiration to any finish carpenter.

Page 3
This fireplace mantel and surround were made by combining several pieces of mitered molding and attaching them to a backing board.

Back Cover
Top left: Wood-turning tools are used in conjunction with a lathe to produce items such as balusters. Other ways to shape wood can be found starting on page 33.
Top right: A jack plane is used for removing large amounts of wood from a straight board. It can be followed up with a smoothing plane. A discussion of planes begins on page 35.
Bottom left: Accurate measuring and marking are the keys to successful finish carpentry. A complete discussion of measuring and marking starts on page 24.
Bottom right: Nails and screws are the most common means of fastening pieces of wood together. Other means of joining wood are discussed starting on page 39.

PORTALIGN is a registered trademark of Portalign Tool Company.
SURFORM is a registered trademark of Stanley Power Tools.

Finish Carpentry Basics

PLOTTING THE COURSE

Building a new house or remodeling an existing one is done in steps. This book deals with the last of these steps—the one that comes after the rough framing is completed; the wiring, plumbing, and heating are roughed in; and the doors, windows, siding, and roofing are in place. In finish carpentry tight joints, clean miters, excellent materials, and smooth surfaces are essential. Although slight inaccuracies and flawed lumber are acceptable in rough carpentry, the success of all the projects in this book depends on working carefully, having patience, taking your time, and choosing materials wisely. Careful planning is equally important. So before you forge ahead, take the time to read through the information presented in this chapter.

Here are just a few of the tools used in the progression from rough framing to finish carpentry.

PLANNING AND SCHEDULING

It is often said that finish carpentry—the final 10 percent of the job—takes as long as all the rest of the job put together. This is largely due to the attention to detail and the exactness that finish work requires. It also calls for accurate information and adequate instruction. Here is what you'll need to know about planning and scheduling—the first steps in finish carpentry.

Stages of Construction

It is important to be familiar not only with finish carpentry but also with all the steps that precede it, since they sometimes overlap. The stages of construction are listed in the order in which they are usually undertaken.

1. Planning. Deciding what to do and how to do it and acquiring the necessary permits

2. Rough carpentry. Laying the foundation and erecting the basic framework

3. Exterior finish carpentry. Cladding the exterior framework with finish materials, installing windows and exterior doors, building exterior stairways and railings, and installing exterior trim

4. Plumbing and wiring. Running lines to all points where power, water, and drainpipes will be needed

5. Heating and cooling. Installing the systems necessary to keep the house comfortable the year around

6. Insulation. Placing batts or rigid insulation in the roof, walls, and floors; making the structure energy efficient

7. Interior finish carpentry. Putting up ceilings and walls, laying floors, building interior stairways and railings, installing cabinets and shelves, and applying interior trim and moldings

8. Decorating. Painting, carpeting, furnishing, and adding the final touches that transform the structure into the home you envisioned

Planning

Successfully completed jobs begin with thoughtful planning; yours will be no exception. Planning is the most important element of a construction project. No amount of adjustment after the fact will make up for a poorly planned job.

Your strategies should be based on a firm grasp of what jobs are to be done and when they must be finished. For example, it is best to complete the exterior of the dwelling before proceeding with the interior, to avoid the construction delays and potential damage to materials that are inevitable with inclement weather. The exterior trim is installed before or after the siding, depending on the type of siding chosen. Interior trim, cabinets, and stairs are installed after other interior construction has been completed. The sequence of activities (see page 64) should be considered at the outset, in order to dovetail each job into the flow of work and achieve maximum efficiency. Once you understand how all the elements in the sequence are interrelated, you will be able to formulate an efficient plan.

Scheduling

Following the correct sequence in any building project is essential for several reasons.

• Building codes demand that inspectors check various aspects of the job. They can make you tear out work if you have proceeded without verification.

• Work that is being subcontracted must be carefully scheduled in order to be time- and cost-effective.

• Poor planning could necessitate dismantling work in order to install items that were overlooked.

• If all the materials that you need aren't on hand, progress can be halted for days, or even weeks, while you wait for deliveries. (Large quantities of lumber as well as manufactured doors, windows, and cabinets should be ordered well ahead of time.)

• Materials can be damaged during construction, so the most visible work should be done last.

Sequence of Events

Finish carpentry starts only after the basic carpentry or remodeling is complete, including everything on the following list.

• Solid foundation
• Girders, sills, and floor joists in place
• Clean, smooth subfloor
• Framework for all doors and windows
• Ceiling joists in place
• Framing, sheathing, and roofing installed
• Stairs roughed in
• Boxes for all switches and outlets nailed to studs
• Outlets for ceiling fixtures nailed to joists
• Gas or electric hookup for oven and cooktop
• Officially approved and inspected wiring
• Officially approved and inspected plumbing lines
• Heating and cooling systems installed and ready for hookup

- Windows and exterior doors in place
- Fully insulated roof, ceilings, floors, and walls
- Effective moisture barrier
- Siding installed
- Floors installed
- Interior doors installed

Review these checklists and the information on the next four pages carefully. If any of the listed items is missing, install it before you proceed. Otherwise you risk having to tear out work so that an inspector can approve the work that is underneath.

Next, draw up the materials takeoffs and correct any flaws in the structure. Takeoffs—lists of materials that can be taken off architectural drawings—let you know what supplies are needed for the job and how much they cost, so you can order them efficiently. A sample floor plan and an accompanying materials takeoff appear on pages 12 and 13.

For a professional-looking job, it is important to correct any flaws that were created in the rough-framing stage before you start the finish work. Door and window openings may not be true; walls may have framing members that need to be straightened. The various corrective measures are addressed at the appropriate points in the following chapters.

Doing It Yourself

"I want to save money" and "Carpentry is my hobby" are the two most common reasons given by people who undertake their own finish work. But there are other reasons that you may not have considered.
- Many houses are built by contractors and developers on speculation ("on spec"). In order to sell the houses as quickly as possible, the builder aims to appeal to broad rather than specific tastes, and nothing unusual is included.
- If you are a gourmet cook, a sound-conscious audiophile, or a collector of porcelain figurines, you may have particular needs that require expensive custom work.
- Ensuring that a home is convenient and comfortable for a person with special needs, such as mobility or sight impairment, poses very particular problems. You know best what specific features are necessary.
- A contracted carpenter will probably not care as much about your home as you do. If you are a perfectionist or a stickler for detail, you are often better off doing the finish work yourself.

Cost

Just how much money can you save by doing your own finish carpentry? It depends on the following variables.
- Cost of local labor
- Cost of supplies in your area

- Size of the project
- Amount of time allotted to complete the project
- Your competence as a finish carpenter
- Difficulty of the job
- Site conditions

The cost of materials and labor varies greatly with the area and with the job site. Materials costs vary from one supplier to the next. Retailers pay fairly consistent wholesale prices; the difference in markup is due mostly to freight costs and local marketing strategies. The best way to economize is to use materials grown or produced in your area.

Some materials are more labor-intensive than others. For example, relative costs for trim might be approximately 40 cents per linear foot for labor if materials cost 60 cents per linear foot; plywood paneling may be 80 cents per square foot for labor if materials are 75 cents per square foot; and wallboard may be 55 cents per square foot if materials are 15 cents per square foot.

Safety Tips

Keep the following suggestions in mind to help the job proceed safely and efficiently.
- Always have a first-aid kit handy at the site, and know how to use it.
- Don't undertake potentially dangerous tasks when working alone at an isolated site.
- Never operate power tools in wet weather or near water.

- Always tuck in loose clothing and tie back long hair, and remove all jewelry when working with hand or power tools.
- Don't risk injuring your back by overestimating the amount of weight you can lift. Remember to lift with your legs, not with your back.
- Wear safety goggles when using a high-speed power tool, or any tool you must raise above your head.
- Wear a particle dust mask and an approved respirator when in contact with airborne materials or toxic chemicals.
- Take your time. Most accidents are the result of taking shortcuts or of not setting up properly.
- Keep the guards on all power equipment. Removing them for convenience could severely injure you.
- Maintain an electrical ground on all power equipment cords.
- Maintain sharp blades on all saws. Dull blades can cause accidents. Keep all blades set at their proper heights.
- Work at a comfortable pace. The potential for injury increases dramatically when you work too fast. (Production is usually more efficient at a reasonable speed, too.)
- Don't work when you are tired or distracted. You're more accident-prone at these times.

PICTORIAL INDEX

Although your house may not look anything like the one pictured here, it probably contains most of the same elements. Each one either is listed in the index of this book or is covered at length in Ortho's Home Improvement Encyclopedia.

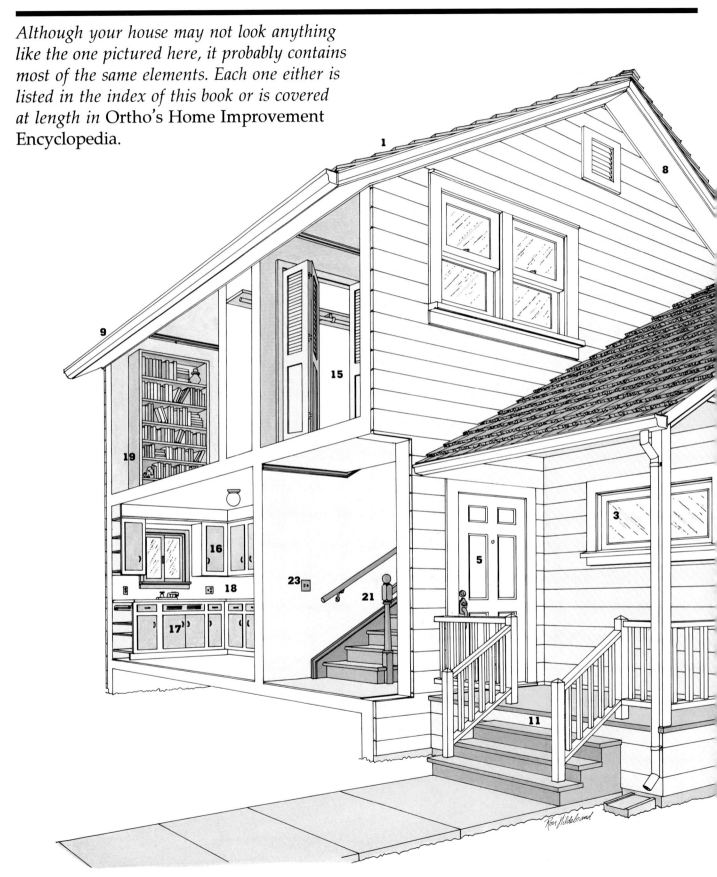

1. Roof. The roofing should be in place.

2. Windows. The windows should be in place.

3. Fixed-pane windows.

4. Exterior window and door trim. Whether the trim goes on before or after the siding depends on the choice of siding material. For when to install window trim and how to measure, cut, and nail it in place, see page 48. For door trim, see page 52.

5. Doors. The doors should be in place.

6. Siding. The siding should be in place.

7. Vents. Attic, basement, and crawl space vents should be in place.

8. Friezes, cornices, and soffits. These make the framing weathertight and add decorative detail. Depending on the amount of overhang, they can also provide shelter while you fumble for keys at the door. See page 53.

9. Gutters and downspouts. A drainage system should already exist. However, you need gutters and downspouts to carry the water from the roof to a storm drain. For how to install them, see page 57.

10. Garage doors. How to trim a garage door is shown on page 52.

11. Exterior stairs and railings. A well-illustrated discussion starts on page 58.

12. Ceilings. Various styles of ceilings and ceiling coverings are discussed in the section that starts on page 65.

13. Wall surfaces. For the most common options—board and sheet paneling and wallboard—see the discussion that starts on page 67.

14. Flooring. The floors should be in place. Installing baseboard is discussed on page 104.

15. Closets. For how to finish traditional, contemporary, multi-purpose, and specific-use closets, see page 79.

16. Wall cabinets. See page 82 for instructions on how to make and install your own wall cabinets, and how to install manufactured units.

17. Base cabinets. It is not difficult to make your own base units. Instructions on how to install these and manufactured units are given on page 84.

18. Countertops. For a discussion on countertops, see *Ortho's Home Improvement Encyclopedia.*

19. Shelves. See page 91 for various methods of mounting shelves.

20. Interior window and door trim. For instructions on measuring, cutting, and installing window trim, see page 95. For door trim see page 99.

21. Interior stairs and railings. For a discussion of interior stairs, railings, balusters, and stair trim, see page 93.

22. Moldings. Whether you use manufactured moldings or shape your own, the method of installation is the same. For information on ceiling trim, picture rails, chair rails, and baseboard, see the section that starts on page 100.

23. Electric cover plates. There's nothing complicated about attaching these.

24. Fireplace mantel and surround. This trim can either be purchased or be made up of pieces of molding assembled in your workshop and then attached in place. See page 106.

THE BASIC SYSTEMS

Make sure that the following systems are in place before you begin finish carpentry. Even people who consider themselves competent carpenters often elect to hire professionals for this work. If you do it yourself, make sure that the local building codes don't specify that the work must be done by certified professionals.

Heating And Cooling

The less easily manipulated elements of the basic systems should be installed first. For example, since it is easier to route an electrical wire around a heating duct or a water pipe than vice versa, the ducts and pipes should be installed first. Route the ducts as directly as possible from the furnace to the registers to obtain maximum heating efficiency. If you are putting in a hot-water, steam, or gas heating system, install the heating pipes at the same time as the plumbing pipes. With electric heat you should install the wiring at the same time as the rest of the house wiring. A cooling system should also be installed and ready to hook up before you apply the finish walls.

Plumbing

In walls with plumbing you should have 2 by 6 studs instead of the usual 2 by 4s, because the studs must be notched to accommodate the pipes. The local building codes will specify how to treat these notches, but keep in mind that you cannot cut completely through a stud, and also that it is good practice to reinforce the stud after installing pipes in

a cutout. You can cut away up to one third of the thickness of a stud. If you cut away two thirds to install the pipe in the middle of the stud (a good way to avoid condensation damage to the wall), you will have to replace and secure the outer third of the stud.

A metal strip should be nailed over the notch to prevent nails from piercing the pipe. If joists are notched for pipes, you can cut no more than one fourth of the thickness of the joist, leaving at least 2 inches of solid wood along the top and bottom edges. Use hangers and braces to support the weight of the plumbing, vent pipes, air chambers, and so on. If the plans call for a built-in bathtub, install it and hook it into the plumbing now. Protect it from damage during construction by leaving on as much shipping material as possible. If a one-piece plastic bathtub enclosure is to be installed, it must be moved into position before the interior walls are completely framed.

In some locales with a severe fire hazard, sprinkler systems may be required in dwellings. These must be in place prior to close-in inspections.

Wiring

Studs drilled to accommodate electrical wiring need not be reinforced, even if they are standard 2 by 4s. The code requires that holes be drilled as close to the center of the studs as possible. If a hole must be drilled close to the edge of a stud, a metal protection plate should be installed where the wiring passes through the stud.

Whether you use plastic cable, spiral armored cable, or thin-wall conduit, install it and connect it to the boxes now. Don't forget that the wiring for the doorbell and the electric burglar and fire alarm systems should be installed as part of the basic wiring. Locate the boxes according to the approved plans, but do not install the switch plates, plugs, or fixtures until after the finish wall surface has been applied. Attach all boxes securely so that you don't end up with wobbly switches and plugs. Nail each box directly to a stud through the top or side flange. If a box must be installed between studs, secure it with an adjustable strap or with supports made for this purpose.

Never do any electrical work unless the circuit is dead. If in doubt, shut off the entire system. When you turn the power back on, check for live or dead circuits using a circuit tester; a small bulb, attached to two probes, lights up if the wire is hot. To test wiring runs, switches, and the like for short circuits and other wiring flaws, use a continuity tester—an inexpensive device that runs off a battery and saves a good deal of fretting. This device should be used only on wires that are not carrying power.

In residential construction it is currently common practice to install telephone, cable TV, fire and burglar alarms, and speaker wires before applying the interior wallcoverings. The installations may be done by the companies providing the service, or in some instances by the owner. If any of these services are included in your project, contact the appropriate agency for particulars.

Insulation

Although you may be eager to install the finish walls so that the house will start to look livable, there is one more major job to do first—installing insulation. This must be done before the interior walls go in but after the heating, rough plumbing, and wiring are complete; the insulation must fit snugly around these elements to be effective. (Remember that a close-in inspection must be done before the insulation can be installed.)

Insulation should always be installed as close to the heated space as possible. This way the furnace isn't heating unused space. For example, if you have an unheated attic, place the insulation between the ceiling joists of the space to be heated rather than between the roof rafters.

A vapor barrier on the warm side of the insulation keeps condensation from forming. Some insulation already has a vapor barrier. If the one you use does not, install an impervious paper or plastic film over the insulation. Attach the barrier to the studs, covering all of your previous work, including the plumbing and

Typical Plumbing

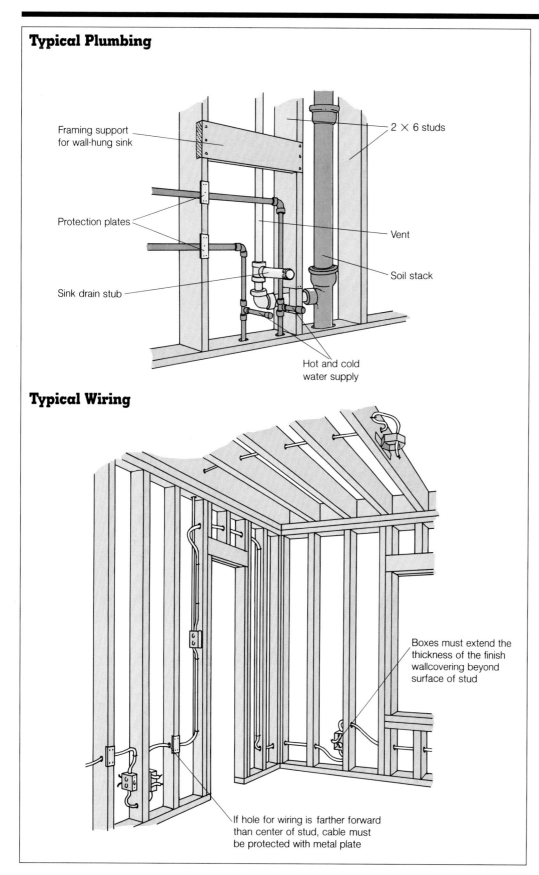

Framing support for wall-hung sink

2 × 6 studs

Protection plates

Vent

Soil stack

Sink drain stub

Hot and cold water supply

Typical Wiring

Boxes must extend the thickness of the finish wallcovering beyond surface of stud

If hole for wiring is farther forward than center of stud, cable must be protected with metal plate

wiring. It is a good idea to stretch the vapor barrier right over the door and window openings to ensure a snug fit. Cut away this extra material when you are ready to install the doors and windows. (In some climates vapor barriers are not commonly used, so check with the local building department for guidelines.)

Energy-Saving Devices

Anyone building a home now-adays should consider installing energy-saving devices. Some that you may want to include are listed below.

• Insulation in the attic, basement, and garage.

• A small air-lock anteroom for heavy-traffic areas that lead outside—back doors used by children, for example. This anteroom can also serve as a mudroom and a place to store boots and raincoats.

• Exterior awnings, to reduce summer heat on the sunny sides of the house. (They should be folded back or removed during the winter.)

• Interior shades and blinds.

• Fans to cool the attic in the summer, as well as fans throughout the house to replace or supplement air-conditioning.

• Siding and insulation enclosing the outside of the fireplace and the chimney to reduce conduction heat loss.

• Ceramic-tile flooring to act as a solar-collection mass.

• Solar-collection panels that are hooked up to the water supply.

• A greenhouse collector in a south-facing window or door opening. The greenhouse can be purchased as a kit or you can design and build your own.

MATERIALS TAKEOFFS

Before you can order materials, you must be able to determine how much of each one is required. This is done by drawing up lists called takeoffs.

Since the cost of finish materials is relatively high, it is wise to calculate the amounts you will need as accurately as possible. It also helps to visualize the completed details of each job, which makes for more efficient ordering and less waste.

Materials takeoffs (see illustration) can be generated by taking off the required amounts from the architectural drawings, or by measuring at the job site, or both. If the drawings truly reflect the actual construction, you can determine the various lengths of materials quickly by using an architect's scale, a ruler that allows you to measure actual dimensions directly on the drawing. It is advisable to visit the job site with tape measure in hand, to verify the figures on the drawings and to take dimensions that are difficult to determine accurately from the drawings. Some lumber and millwork companies will do the takeoffs for you from your plans and provide you with a list and a quote on the price of materials.

In finish carpentry, materials are divided into two categories: those that are ordered and installed in random lengths, such as baseboard, chair rail, picture rail, and crown molding—and those that are ordered in specific lengths for a particular application, such as door and window casings, wainscoting frames, shelves, stair treads, and railings.

Materials in random, or running, lengths are ordered and delivered to the job site in whatever lengths are available. For example, baseboard stock, ordered in random lengths, may arrive at the site in sections varying from 4 to 16 feet. The total count, say 450 linear feet, would come from the sum of all the individual room measurements using that type of baseboard, plus about 10 percent to allow for waste and errors in cutting.

Materials ordered in specific, or standing, lengths are installed at the particular locations for which they are ordered. In this instance, you would order exterior door casings as follows. For a standard door height of 6 feet 8 inches, the side casing material is 7 feet long and the head casing approximately 3 feet long. The sum of these lengths is 17 feet. Noting that the material is sold in multiples of 2 feet, you would order an 18-foot length. From this installation you would have about 1 foot of waste material.

This method works primarily for exterior door (and window) casings. The drawback for ordering interior door casings is that 18-foot lengths of interior casing are often special-order items, so the savings in waste may be more than offset by the premium price of the material. A better method, with less waste, for interior door and window casings is as follows. For doors, order three 14-foot lengths of casing and you will get four 7-foot side casings and two 3-foot head casings, enough for both sides of one door, with one 7-foot side casing left over for the next door. This reduces the waste to less

Materials Takeoff List for Room Addition

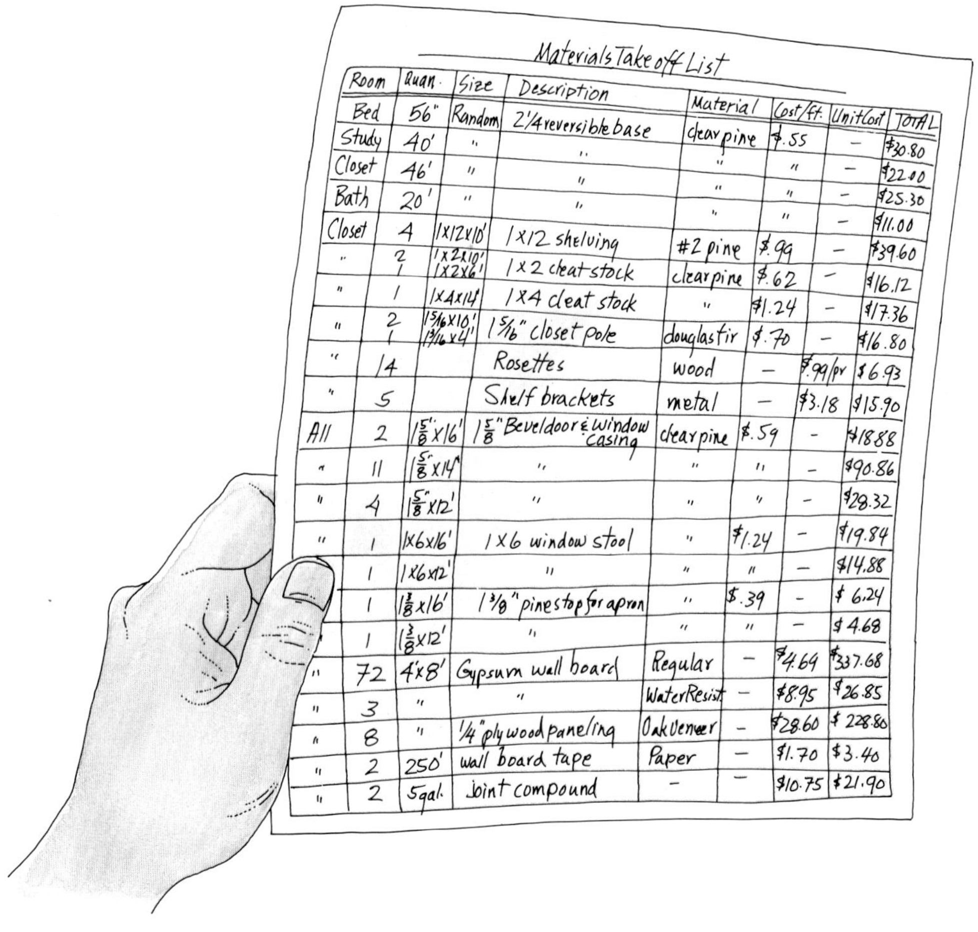

Materials Take off List

Room	Quan.	Size	Description	Material	Cost/Ft.	Unit Cost	TOTAL
Bed	56'	Random	2¼ reversible base	clear pine	$.55	–	$30.80
Study	40'	"	"	"	"	–	$22.00
Closet	46'	"	"	"	"	–	$25.30
Bath	20'	"	"	"	"	–	$11.00
Closet	4	1x12x10'	1x12 shelving	#2 pine	$.99	–	$39.60
"	2 1	1x2x10' 1x2x6'	1x2 cleat stock	clear pine	$.62	–	$16.12
"	1	1x4x14'	1x4 cleat stock	"	$1.24	–	$17.36
"	2 1	1 5/16x10' 1 3/16x4'	1 5/16" closet pole	douglas fir	$.70	–	$16.80
"	14		Rosettes	wood	–	$.99/pr	$6.93
"	5		Shelf brackets	metal	–	$3.18	$15.90
All	2	1 5/8x16'	1 5/8" Bevel door & window casing	clear pine	$.59	–	$18.88
"	11	1 5/8x14'	"	"	"	–	$90.86
"	4	1 5/8x12'	"	"	"	–	$28.32
"	1	1x6x16'	1x6 window stool	"	$1.24	–	$19.84
	1	1x6x12'	"	"	"	–	$14.88
	1	1 3/8x16'	1 3/8" pinestop for apron	"	$.39	–	$6.24
	1	1 3/8x12'	"	"	"	–	$4.68
"	72	4'x8'	Gypsum wall board	Regular	–	$4.69	$337.68
"	3	"	"	Water Resist	–	$8.95	$26.85
"	8	"	1/4" plywood paneling	Oak Veneer	–	$28.60	$228.80
"	2	250'	wall board tape	Paper	–	$1.70	$3.40
"	2	5 gal.	joint compound	–	–	$10.75	$21.90

than 1 foot per door. If the casings aren't available in 14-foot lengths, two 10-foot lengths and two 8-foot lengths will do, although this will yield two 1-foot sections of waste material per door.

When ordering other finish carpentry materials, such as shelves and closet poles, stair treads, risers, and railings, a method similar to standing length is used to calculate the amounts. The length of each item is determined and then multiplied by the number of those items. For example, if you have six shelves to install and each is to be 2 feet 6 inches long, 6 × 2½ feet = 15 feet.

Order a 16-foot piece of shelf stock, or one 10-foot piece and one 6-foot piece.

When ordering wallboard and paneling, you must calculate areas to determine the amounts. Calculations for wallboard are done as follows. Measure the widths, lengths, and heights of the wall and ceiling surfaces. Multiply these to obtain the area of each surface. Sum up the surface areas to find the total area. Divide this total by the area of one sheet to determine the total number of sheets required.

For example, let's say a room is 20 feet long and 16 feet wide, with an 8-foot ceiling.

Two walls are 20 feet long; 2 × 20 feet = 40 feet. Two walls are 16 feet long; 2 × 16 feet = 32 feet. Adding these together gives 72 feet. Multiplying by the height—8 feet—gives 576 square feet of wall surface.

The ceiling is 20 feet by 16 feet, for 320 square feet of ceiling surface. Adding 576 square feet to 320 square feet gives a total area of 896 square feet. Dividing this by 32 square feet (the area of a 4 by 8 sheet of wallboard) gives 28. This is the number of sheets to purchase. Do not reduce the total area by the areas of the door and window openings, unless these openings are 8 feet or more in

height (the length of a sheet of wallboard). You may reduce the total area for the floor-to-ceiling openings between rooms. Add a couple of sheets to the count for botched cuts and breakage.

Professional installers often use 4 by 12 sheets of wallboard to speed up the job. If you choose to do that too, your factor for dividing total square footage will be 48 (4 × 12) rather than 32. A helpful hint: Do not attempt to install 12-foot sheets by yourself.

Calculations for 4 by 8 paneling are done sheet by sheet. This is because ceilings are not usually paneled, and because paneling, unlike wallboard, is usually used in only one or two rooms of a house. So, for example, if a room measures 20 feet by 16 feet, the total length for four walls is 72 feet. Dividing this by 4 feet (the width of a sheet of paneling) gives 18. This is the number of sheets to purchase, assuming that the height of the room is 8 feet. As with wallboard, reduce the number of sheets only if there are large openings.

Board paneling is usually sold in packages that will cover a given area, such as 32 square feet. If the height of the room is 8 feet, the contents of the latter package will cover 4 linear feet of wall. The material in the package may vary in length from 1 foot to 8 feet, so if you must install nailing surfaces (called cleats) before applying the paneling, remember to determine the proper spacing for the cleats. Be sure to order about 10 percent extra material to allow for waste and errors.

Floor Plan for Room Addition

CHOOSING THE MATERIALS

The right materials for the job ensure both permanence and economy. The choice is easier if you study the charts showing the characteristics of the various materials (see pages 17 to 21), and if you familiarize yourself with the illustrations showing how lumber is cut and graded (see pages 15 and 16).

Sources of Information

A wide variety of materials is used in finish carpentry. Knowing the useful characteristics of each will pay handsome dividends. Choosing the right materials, like choosing the right tool, makes any job easier and more satisfying. In addition, knowing the characteristics of the various materials will help you to achieve the look you want in any finished project, whether it's soffits under the eaves or fine cabinets in the kitchen. By shopping carefully you can select materials that are cost efficient, durable, attractive, and easy to maintain.

Apart from the charts and information given in this chapter, there are other sources that you can turn to for help.

Make use of the local library. Because do-it-yourself projects are so popular, even small libraries stock a good selection of reference books. Look through them and make a list of titles that might be worth buying for your own library.

Home-building magazines are a gold mine of information and ideas. Study the advertisements as well as the articles. Many contain coupons for catalogs and brochures, some of which are quite lavish. They

are usually offered free or for a nominal charge.

Check the stores in your area, not only for materials but also for ready-made products that will save time. For example, staircases can be ordered to your specifications. If you need a railing for a porch or balcony, look for stores that carry a variety of decorative balusters. Ornamental moldings come in styles that range from simple plastic cove strips to elaborate turned-wood caps.

When you find a good store, try to establish a relationship with the sales staff. In most stores these people are very knowledgeable, and you can save time and mistakes by enlisting their aid. Don't be afraid to ask questions. As long as you don't arrive on a busy Saturday morning, these professionals will usually be happy to help. If they aren't, shop elsewhere.

Maintaining Architectural Style

The style of a house, whether Cape Cod, Georgian, or modern, is emphasized by the finish carpentry. The trim, doors, and windows give a house its character. In most instances,

the style is dictated by the architectural drawings, leaving little or no latitude for spontaneous creative expression during the finish phase. If you have some flexibility in the selection of materials, however, consider the options carefully. It is important to maintain an overall look that is harmonious and aesthetically pleasing and is in keeping with the intent of the design.

Nonwood Trim

Many materials besides wood are used to make trim; they include plastic, resin, rubber, metal, and vinyl.

Plastic trim, a high-density polystyrene or polyurethane foam, is manufactured in various shapes, from simple straight pieces, such as baseboards, corners, casings, and chair and picture rails, to complex architectural elements, such as pilasters, mantels, and pediments. The materials cost for some designs may be higher than it would be for wood trim, but this cost is usually more than offset by the savings in labor. Plastic trim is easily cut, fit, and nailed, dramatically reducing production and installation time. Some styles don't even have to be painted.

Also available are lightweight moldings made from a flexible resin; they can be used in places where conventional wood trim cannot be easily bent to fit. These moldings are expensive, but they may be the most practical solution to a difficult installation problem.

Some nonwood base trim is made of rubber or vinyl. It is used primarily with sheet vinyl or vinyl tile finish floors. Trim

pieces made of vinyl are available for finishing exterior vinyl siding installations. They come in a variety of shapes and styles.

Metal trim is occasionally used in exterior applications. Most commonly it is installed at outside corners when the house is finished with a type of wood siding known as bevel. This closes off the board ends to the weather, which minimizes deterioration.

Selecting Wood

Mill and lumberyard personnel have a language all their own. Knowing the correct terminology eliminates costly mistakes when ordering, and it cuts down on your shopping time.

Dimensioned lumber is 2 or more inches thick (nominal). It is used for ordinary framing, and it includes the ubiquitous 2 by 4 as well as 2 by 6, 2 by 8, and 4-by lumber. Timber is lumber 5 by 5 and larger. It is used for heavy framing—in car decks, for example. Board lumber is less than 2 inches thick. It is not structurally strong enough to be used for framing. Along with plywood and milled wood products it is used for sheathing, siding, subfloors, casings, and trim. The most common board lumber is 1 inch (actually ¾ inch) thick and 2 to 12 inches wide.

From Trees to Lumber

At the sawmill logs are cut into lumber or veneer by one of three methods. (See illustration on page 16.)

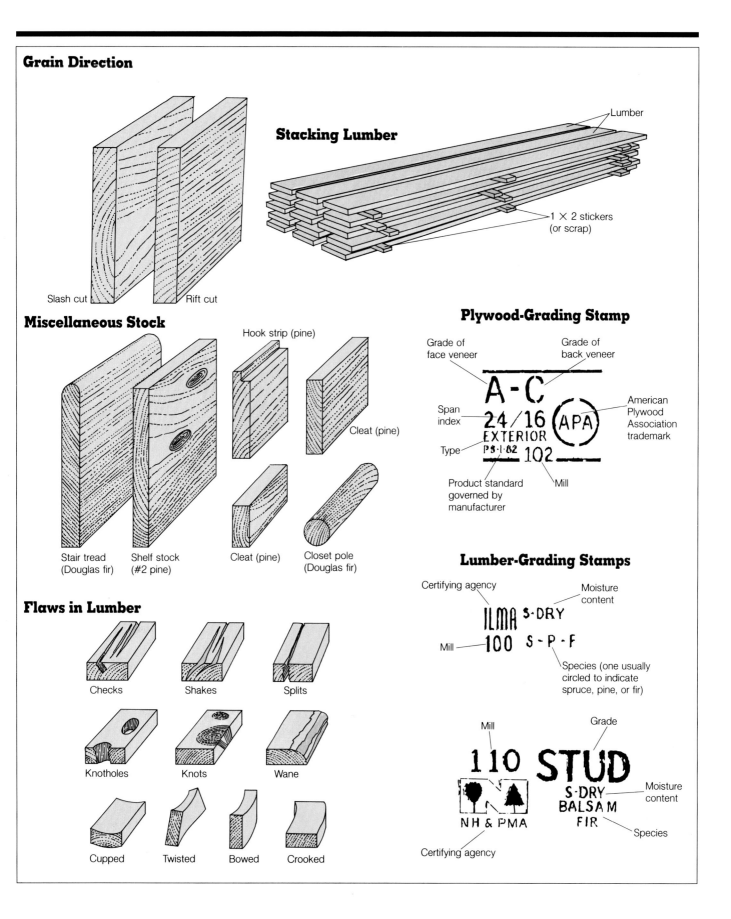

Grain Direction

Stacking Lumber

Lumber

1 × 2 stickers (or scrap)

Slash cut

Rift cut

Miscellaneous Stock

Hook strip (pine)

Cleat (pine)

Stair tread (Douglas fir)

Shelf stock (#2 pine)

Cleat (pine)

Closet pole (Douglas fir)

Flaws in Lumber

Checks

Shakes

Splits

Knotholes

Knots

Wane

Cupped

Twisted

Bowed

Crooked

Plywood-Grading Stamp

Grade of face veneer

Grade of back veneer

A-C
24/16 (APA)
EXTERIOR
PS-1-82 102

Span index

Type

American Plywood Association trademark

Product standard governed by manufacturer

Mill

Lumber-Grading Stamps

Certifying agency

Moisture content

ILMA S-DRY
100 S-P-F

Mill

Species (one usually circled to indicate spruce, pine, or fir)

Mill

Grade

110 STUD
S-DRY
BALSAM
FIR

NH & PMA

Moisture content

Species

Certifying agency

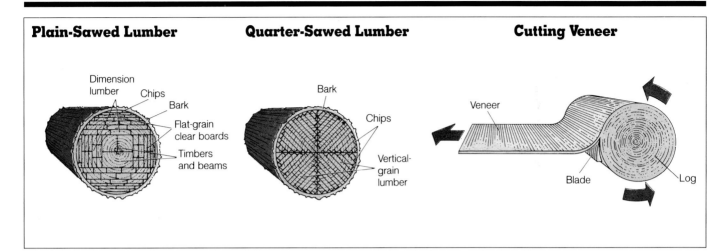

Plain-Sawed Lumber

Dimension lumber
Chips
Bark
Flat-grain clear boards
Timbers and beams

Quarter-Sawed Lumber

Bark
Chips
Vertical-grain lumber

Cutting Veneer

Veneer
Blade
Log

Plain Sawed

Most construction-grade (dimension) lumber used for studs, joists, and rafters is plain sawed. This method is the fastest, and it produces relatively little waste, so the lumber is usually inexpensive. The slash cuts (see illustration on page 15) produce boards with surfaces unsuited to finish work, because the pronounced grain fissures show as marbling or as dark U or oval shapes. Plain-sawed lumber is also more prone to warping than quarter-sawed lumber.

Quarter Sawed

These boards are produced by rift cuts—that is, the annual rings of the log run perpendicular to the cut surface. This gives the board a finer grain than is possible with plain-sawed lumber. It also exposes the denser summerwood rings more evenly across the surface, so the wood is more durable.

Because this method wastes more of the original log, quarter-sawed lumber is more expensive than plain-sawed lumber, but it is the better choice in finish carpentry, where appearance and durability are important.

Veneer

Most veneers are produced by mounting a log on a huge lathelike machine and shaving off a thin slice of the outer surface as the log spins. As the shaver blade moves toward the axis of the log, it produces a thin, continuous sheet. Some veneers are plain sawed or quarter sawed, however, to create special grain effects. Most veneers are used in the manufacture of laminated wood products, such as wood paneling and plywood; unlaminated veneers made of fine woods are used in cabinetmaking.

Moisture Content

Woods used for finish carpentry should contain 19 percent or less of moisture. This figure corresponds to the standard grade called S-DRY. Moisture content is particularly important if you live in a dry climate, because wood shrinks as it loses moisture. For very exacting finish carpentry, select wood that is graded MC-15 (15 percent or less moisture content). For cabinetwork and furniture making, select wood that is graded MC-10 or MC-12.

Quality

Be on the lookout for defects. As wood seasons, a small split can widen into an unsightly blemish. Products such as moldings and window casings are made of select wood. If you buy unmilled stock and do your own shaping, make sure that it is of good quality.

When ordering large quantities of lumber, see if you can buy a percentage lot. This is construction-grade lumber with some appearance-grade lumber mixed in. You have to sort out the higher-grade boards yourself, but you stand to save substantially on the wood that you ultimately use for trim.

Stacking and Storing

Wood that is to be used for finish work should be stored flat. Stack the material off the ground in a dry area. Short lengths of 1 by 2 make ideal supports. (Lumberyards call them stickers.) Set the supports close enough together so that the boards do not sag. Every few layers place more stickers crosswise to stabilize the stack and allow air to circulate.

Choosing Wood Species

Selecting the right wood for a particular job is part of design and planning. Know what materials are available in your area before you start to build.

Check with local suppliers regarding availability, ordering time, and cost. Not all lumberyards carry unusual species of wood. Check the yellow pages to find specialty suppliers in your area. The chart on page 17 rates a number of common hardwoods and softwoods used in finish carpentry. Consult one of the many books on wood for further information.

Hardness and Strength

The terms *hardwood* and *softwood* are confusing since they do not indicate the actual hardness and softness of a wood. Yellow pine, for example, is a softwood that is actually harder than mahogany, which is classified as a hardwood. The term *hardwood* refers largely to deciduous trees, which lose their leaves in the fall; the term *softwood* refers to coniferous

Woods for Finish Carpentry

Wood Species	Hardness	Strength	Cutting Quality	Planing Quality	Gluing Quality	Stain Recommended	Suitable for Painting?
Ash	Medium	Medium	Poor	Medium	Poor	Any	Yes, heavy filler
Basswood	Poor	Poor	Good	Good	Good	Water	Yes, no filler
Beech	Good	Medium	Medium	Medium	Medium	Water	Yes, thin filler
Birch	Good	Good	Medium	Medium	Poor	Any	Yes, thin filler
Cedar (w. red)	Poor	Poor	Good	Medium	Good	Oil	Yes, no filler
Cherry	Medium	Medium	Good	Good	Medium	Water	No, thin filler
Cypress	Poor	Medium	Medium	Medium	Medium	Oil	Yes, no filler
Douglas fir	Medium	Medium	Medium	Poor	Good	Oil	Yes, no filler
Elm (Amer.)	Medium	Medium	Medium	Poor	Medium	Water	Yes, heavy filler
Gum (sweet, red)	Medium	Medium	Good	Medium	Good	Any	Yes, thin filler
Hard maple	Good	Good	Poor	Medium	Poor	Any	Yes, thin filler
Hemlock	Medium	Medium	Medium	Poor	Good	Oil	Yes, no filler
Hickory	Good	Good	Poor	Medium	Medium	Water	No, heavy filler
Mahogany	Medium	Medium	Medium	Medium	Good	Water	No, medium filler
Ponderosa pine	Poor	Poor	Good	Good	Good	Any	Yes, no filler
Red oak	Good	Good	Poor	Medium	Medium	Water	Yes, heavy filler
Redwood	Poor	Medium	Good	Medium	Good	Oil	Yes, no filler
Soft maple	Medium	Medium	Medium	Poor	Medium	Any	Yes, thin filler
Spruce	Poor	Poor	Good	Good	Good	Any	Yes, no filler
Teak	Good	Good	Dulls tools quickly	Good	Poor	Any	No, heavy filler
Walnut	Medium	Good	Good	Good	Good	Water	No, medium filler
White oak	Good	Good	Poor	Medium	Medium	Water	Yes, heavy filler
Yellow pine	Medium	Good	Medium	Good	Medium	Any	Yes, no filler

trees, such as pines, which retain their leaves (needles) the year around.

Stair treads and flooring, which must withstand heavy use, are usually made of hardwoods, such as oak and maple. Some softwoods, however, such as Douglas fir in quarter-sawn form, and yellow pine, are hard enough and strong enough to be acceptable.

Handrails, balusters, and built-in furniture, which must be able to support weight and withstand years of wear, are often made of hardwood. Softwood is often used for vertical surfaces that do not suffer heavy wear, such as board siding and trim.

Cutting Quality

The fibers of woods with a spongy texture or very large pores will collapse and deform as the wood is cut. This produces a cut with a rough end grain and many bent or broken fibers. Using appropriate and sharp tools improves the quality of cuts in any wood.

Planing Quality

Even grain planes the most smoothly. Porous hardwoods and soft woods with uneven grain are the most difficult to plane. Always work in the uphill direction. See illustration on page 36, bottom.

Gluing Quality

Most woods can be joined successfully with any one of a variety of glues. Very dense close-grained hardwoods, uneven porous woods, and oily woods are more difficult to glue than softwoods and even-grained woods.

Stain or Paint?

Certain woods, when treated with stain, have a deep, rich color and a well-defined grain. These woods should be stained rather than painted. Other woods may also be stained, however. Do not use varnish, which has an oil base, over an oil-based stain, because the stain will dissolve, lift, and cloud the varnish. Instead use shellac or lacquer.

For smooth painted surfaces, prepare open-pored woods with a filler. On all woods, sand well and apply a sealer or primer before painting.

Selecting Materials

Listed in the following charts are many of the materials commonly used in finish carpentry. Although the store or the lumberyard should be able to answer your questions, shopping will be easier if you make some preliminary decisions. These should be based on aesthetic considerations, permanence, and ease of installation.

Ordering Materials

Material	Stock Item?	Comments
Cabinets	Seldom	Order custom cabinets from a local cabinetmaker, home-improvement center, or manufacturer's representative.
Lumber	Yes	Availability varies. Check on stock, especially for large orders.
Mantel and fireplace surround	Some	Some home-improvement centers carry mantels or will order them for you (delivery times vary). Local cabinetmakers or carpenters will custom-build. (Ask to see samples of their work before ordering.)
Moldings	Some	A good selection of softwood moldings is available at most lumberyards. Many lumberyards now also stock a variety of hardwood and nonwood moldings. For hardwood moldings and/or special designs, check hardwood outlets in your area. Look in magazines for manufacturers who specialize in moldings or order from local millwork shops or cabinetmakers.
Staircases	No	Some home-improvement centers will order a staircase for you (delivery times vary). Local cabinetmakers or carpenters will custom-build. (Ask to see samples of their work before ordering.)
Wallboard	Yes	Although standard and waterproof panels are readily available, decorative ones must usually be ordered.

Sandpaper

Type	Indication of Grades	Uses	Comments
Flint	0000 = very fine, 0 = medium, 3 = very coarse	Removing finishes	Inexpensive paper but clogs easily. Requires frequent replacement.
Garnet	400 = superfine, 220 = very fine, 80 = medium	Sanding wood	Pinkish orange in color. Cuts better than flint and lasts up to 5 times longer.
Aluminum oxide	600 = superfine, 220 = very fine, 80 = medium	Sanding wood, metal, and plastics	Very long lasting. Available in sheet, belt, and disk form.

Sometimes the backing on the sandpaper is as important as the sandpaper itself.

Grade of Backing	Backing Material	Comments
A	Lightweight paper	Backs fine-grit sandpapers. Good for sanding molded or carved surfaces, because it bends easily.
C, D	Medium-weight papers	Also called cabinet papers, these back medium-grit sandpapers. Use C for curved surfaces and D for flat work.
J	Lightweight cloth	Better than paper for wet sanding. Use on curved, shaped, or flat surfaces.
X	Medium-weight cloth	Use for heavy-duty sanding on flat or curved surfaces. Also available as belts and disks for power sanding tools.

Materials for Finish Carpentry

Material	Type	Description	Uses
Abrasives	Paper backed	Available in sheets, belts, or disks, with flint (quick to dull), garnet (general-grade), and aluminum oxide (high-grade) abrasives.	Surfacing (see page 35 for specifics)
	Cloth backed	Stronger backing than paper on the same abrasives as above. Suitable for wet sanding.	Surfacing (see page 35 for specifics)
	Grinding wheels	For general sharpening use a 60-grit aluminum oxide medium-grade wheel. Set speed at 5,000 to 6,000 surface feet per minute (circumference of wheel in feet $\times$ RPM = surface feet per minute).	Sharpening tools
Adhesives	Hide glue	Granules must be dissolved in warm water and glue kept warm while using. Glue pots and brushes are available for this purpose.	Gluing joints and veneers
	Powdered casein	Mix 15 minutes before using. Glue is somewhat water-resistant.	Gluing oily woods, such as teak and yew
	White polyvinyl resin glue	This water-based white glue is inexpensive. It sets quickly and dries clear but is not waterproof. Widely available in squeeze bottles. Clamp work while glue sets.	Multipurpose
	Contact cement	A flammable and noxious solvent. Coat both surfaces to be joined, then let the cement dry (approximately 10 minutes); material will bond on contact. Clamping is not necessary. Contact cement is water-resistant.	Bonding veneers and laminates
	Mastic cement	This puttylike adhesive is available in cans (spread with a trowel) or cartridges (apply with a caulking gun). Some but not all mastics are waterproof.	Adhering materials to vertical and horizontal surfaces
	Resorcinol	A catalyst (two-component) glue for use in high-moisture situations.	Kitchen and bathroom cabinet construction, outdoor projects
	Epoxy	A catalyst glue especially well suited to join wood to other materials.	Adhering wood to glass or metal
	Yellow aliphatic resin glue	Slower setting and more heat resistant than white polyvinyl resin glue.	General-purpose glue
Caulks	Polyvinyl acetate (PVA) latex	Paintable, relatively inflexible material with poor adhesion. Not waterproof. Economical. Water used for cleanup.	Filling gaps and cracks on interior surfaces
	Siliconized acrylic latex	Paintable, flexible material with good adhesion. Generally water-resistant on vertical surfaces. Moderately long lasting. Moderately priced. Water used for cleanup.	Filling gaps and cracks and sealing joints on interior and exterior surfaces
	Silicone rubber	Nonpaintable, flexible material with good adhesion. Waterproof on vertical surfaces. Very long lasting. Good for extreme temperature range. Expensive. III Trichloroethane or paint thinner used for cleanup.	Weatherproofing and sealing joints on exterior surfaces
	Polyurethane	Paintable, flexible material with excellent adhesion. Waterproof under all conditions. Excellent durability. Critical disadvantage: poor shelf life. Moderate to high cost. III Trichloroethane or paint thinner used for cleanup.	Sealing joints and filling gaps on exterior surfaces where moisture exposure is high
	Block copolymer rubber	Paintable, flexible material with excellent adhesion. Waterproof on vertical surfaces. Moderately long lasting. Expensive. III Trichloroethane or paint thinner used for cleanup.	Weatherproofing and sealing joints on exterior surfaces

Materials for Finish Carpentry (continued)

Material	Type	Description	Uses
Fillers	Liquid	Oil-based heavy liquid. Thin with turpentine, tint as needed with powdered colors (mixed first with linseed oil). Paint on with a brush, scrub off with burlap (rub across the grain), sand when dry.	Small-pored woods, such as birch, maple, and cherry
	Paste	Oil-based paste either natural or tinted. Thin with turpentine. Additive available to speed drying time. Trowel filler onto wood, scrape off excess, rub across grain with burlap, sand when dry.	Large-pored woods, such as oak, mahogany, and ash
Finishes	Oil paint	Any of various opaque pigments suspended in linseed oil or, more commonly, alkyd resin. Although flat finishes are available, oil-based paint is mostly used where a gloss finish is required. Clean applicators with turpentine or mineral spirits.	Painting trim and kitchen and bathroom walls
	Latex paint	Synthetic rubber (latex) particles suspended in a water base. Less expensive than oil paint. Clean applicators with water.	General painting
	Varnish	Varnish is oil paint without the pigments. The type of resin used determines the properties of the varnish. Polyurethane is recommended for most uses; it can be brushed or sprayed on and dries clear and hard. Check labels on different varnishes for properties that meet your specific requirements. Clean applicators with mineral spirits.	Finishing water-based–stained wood floors and cabinets
	Shellac	Fast-drying clear finish. Use orange shellac over dark or stained wood; white shellac over light wood. Several coats produce a high-gloss finish, which can be dulled by rubbing with steel wool. Clean applicators with ammonia and water or alcohol.	Finishing oil- or water-based–stained wood floors and cabinets
	Lacquer	Moderately fast drying clear finish. Highly flammable. Dries very hard; resists water, stain, and chemicals. Clean applicators with ammonia and water, or alcohol.	Finishing sealed and unstained cabinets
	Sealer	Oil-based or water-based substance used to fill and seal wood grain, usually before hard-finish material is applied. Clean applicators with turpentine or mineral spirits (oil-based sealer) or water (water-based sealer).	Sealing cabinets and flooring; prevents stains and knots from bleeding through finish; makes sanding easier
	Wax	Melted mixture of beeswax and paraffin, or similar but solidified commercial mixture, which protects wood surfaces. Can be discolored by some substances, so hard-finish material is advised.	Finishing cabinets and other interior wood surfaces
	Stain	Oil-based stain is a suitable exterior finish and preservative for natural wood siding. Water-based stain is used to darken and color interior wood. Apply to clean, unfinished wood.	Protecting and coloring wood
Lumber	Board	Nominally 1 inch thick (actually ¾ inch). Ranges from 2 to 12 inches wide in 2-inch increments. Available up to 16 feet long. Grades are: select, appearance, construction, standard, utility, and economy. (Surfaced on all 4 sides = S4S.)	Shelving, subfloors, trim
	Dimension	Lumber up to 5 inches thick and from 2 to 12 inches wide. Same grading system as for board lumber.	Framing, closet and cabinet construction

Materials for Finish Carpentry (continued)

Material	Type	Description	Uses
Molding		Usually made of clear pine, although hardwood moldings are available. Different suppliers carry different ranges, so check around for a complete selection or order from specialty suppliers.	Baseboard, ceiling molding, picture rail, chair rail, door and window casing, stools, sills, aprons
Paneling	Board	Usually applied vertically. Available in various widths with tongue-and-groove edges. Face can be smooth or V-grooved.	Finish walls
	Sheet	4 by 8 panels with a veneered (often hardwood) face. The large variety of styles includes smooth, textured, or grooved surfaces. Use ⅜-inch panels directly over studs; ¼-inch panels over backer board. Edges are butted (cover seams with battens) or lapped.	Finish walls
Plywood	Interior	Usually all softwood. 4 by 8 panels range from ¼ inch to 1¼ inches thick and have from 3 to 7 plies. The quality and finish of the outer plies determine the grade: A (best), D (worst). (A-C plywood = grade A on one side, grade C on the other. N = hardwood faced.) Edges are squared, shiplapped, or tongue and groove.	Finish walls, cabinets, cabinet doors
	Exterior	Faced with either smooth veneer (grades A through D) or rough sawn. Sometimes the face is grooved for appearance (T-111). Edges can be squared, shiplapped, or tongue and groove.	Siding, exterior trim
	Lumber core	Usually an appearance-grade (N) plywood. Core consists of edge-glued strips of wood.	Cabinetwork
Veneers	Wood	Softwoods and hardwoods available in sheets, strips, rolls, and thin edging strips. Edging strips are sometimes adhesive backed.	Finish surfaces
	Plastic laminate	A long-wearing material that is heat and stain resistant. Available in panels 4 feet wide and up to 10 feet long, in many colors with gloss or matte finishes.	Kitchen and bathroom countertops
Wallboard	Gypsum	Sheets are 4 feet wide and up to 16 feet long (8 feet is standard). The gypsum core is sandwiched between layers of paper. Both standard and waterproof versions usually have tapered edges, although beveled, round, square, and tongue-and-groove edges are also available. Common thicknesses are ¼, ⅜, ½, ⅝ (standard), and ¾ inch.	Wallcovering
Wood products	Hardboard	Pulverized mill waste compressed into 4 by 8 sheets ⅛ inch to ⅜ inch thick. Known as pegboard when surfaced with holes.	Cabinet backs
	Particleboard and waferboard (low-grade)	Wood chips compressed into 4 by 8 sheets ¼ inch to 1½ inches thick. Light tan in color. Quality depends on density.	Cabinet construction, underlayment for countertops and finish floors
	Particleboard (laminated)	High-pressure, laminate-coated particleboard. Scratch and stain resistant. Available from ¼ inch to 1 inch thick. Stock colors are white and tan; other colors can be special-ordered.	Cabinet and draw construction

GAINING THE SKILLS

If you absolutely had to, you could probably build your home with no tools other than a handsaw, a hammer, and a ruler. By utilizing the wide variety of tools available today, however, you can build a better structure and build it faster and more easily. Acquaint yourself with the proper tools and learn how to use them. The right tool for the job is a joy; the wrong tool can be pure frustration.

The tools you need will depend on the projects you are undertaking. Buy tools from hardware stores, lumberyards, and mail-order suppliers. Keep an eye out for new tools on the market. Buy the best tools you can afford; you may pay more for them, but they will last longer and perform more reliably. Books are also valuable tools. Check to see what is available before you start the project. The techniques and tools used in finish carpentry are described on the following pages.

A well-stocked workshop includes a combination of hand and power tools, a workbench, and a tool box ready to take to the job site.

MEASURING AND MARKING

Measuring is the key to success in every carpentry project. Measuring requires no strength or fancy tools—just common sense and concentration. Think about what you are doing and double-check your measurements. You will save time, save waste, and save yourself from doing sloppy—or even dangerous—work.

Measuring the Building

Much finish carpentry simply consists of fitting boards and panels onto the part of the structure that is already completed. To ensure that the finish work covers the framing without overlapping or leaving gaps, take the initial measurements from the framing. You may need a 50-foot or 100-foot tape to measure the length of a fascia board, for example. For most measurements a 16-foot steel tape should be sufficient. The hook on the end of the tape makes it possible for you to work alone.

A few situations call for more specialized tools. Measuring the inside opening of a window frame, for example, is easy if you use a folding rule with an extension slide. To measure the thickness of a board, panel, or piece of molding, a caliper is handy. Some bench rules have a caliper built into one end. Some measuring and marking tools you'll need for finish carpentry are shown in the photograph below.

Don't assume that walls, floors, and ceilings are square and plumb. A wall that measures 14 feet 6 inches at the baseboard may be 14 feet 6½

The measuring and marking tools shown below include (1) carpenter's level, (2) scribe, (3) combination square, (4) try square, (5) wood caliper, (6) sliding bevel, (7) folding rule, (8) plumb bob, (9) steel tape measure, (10) protractor, (11) steel outside caliper, (12) marking gauge, (13) stud finder, (14) torpedo level, (15) steel rule, (16) trammel points mounted on a yardstick, and (17) framing square.

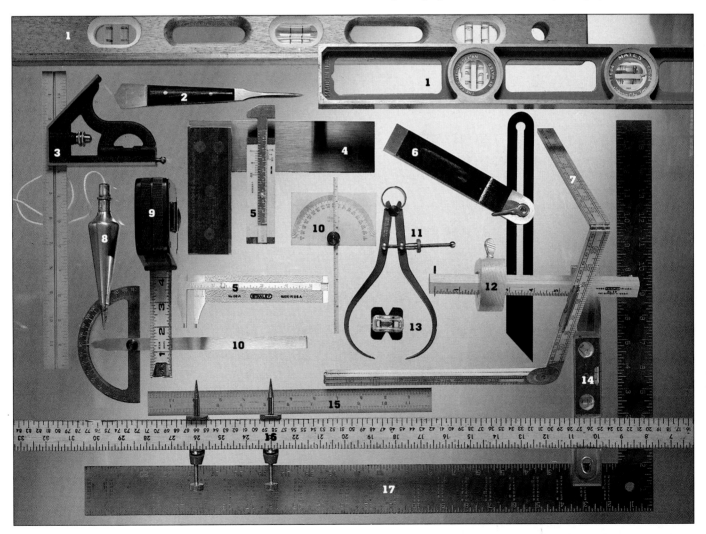

Marking and Cutting

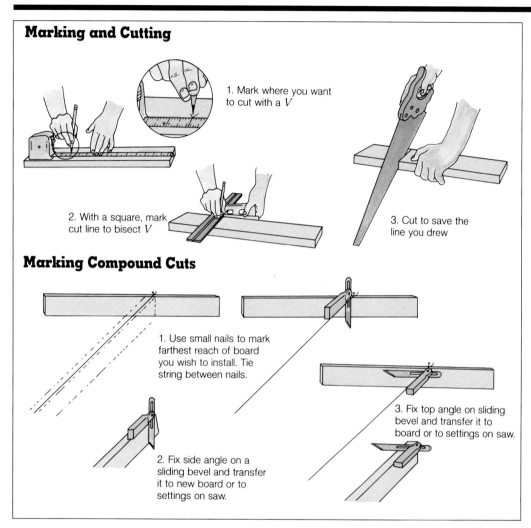

1. Mark where you want to cut with a *V*

2. With a square, mark cut line to bisect *V*

3. Cut to save the line you drew

Marking Compound Cuts

1. Use small nails to mark farthest reach of board you wish to install. Tie string between nails.

2. Fix side angle on a sliding bevel and transfer it to new board or to settings on saw.

3. Fix top angle on sliding bevel and transfer it to board or to settings on saw.

inches at the ceiling. To cope with this unevenness or to correct it, use a plumb bob or a spirit level. A 24-inch carpenter's level, which is the most versatile size, can also be used to even picture rail, chair rail, and door and window casing. When you work with smaller pieces of trim, such as balusters, use a torpedo level.

Measuring at the eaves and around stairways entails transferring angles onto your work. To determine the degrees in an angle, use a steel protractor with a swivel arm. If you simply need to transfer the angle, a sliding bevel is simple to use

and will hold a setting for repeated markings.

Measuring and Laying Out Boards

Measuring the boards themselves is just as important as measuring where they will go. First, don't assume that the boards are square. They probably were cut square at the mill, but lumber often distorts as it dries, and there will usually be checks (cracks) at the ends, which must be trimmed off. Start by cutting off one end of

the first board in ½-inch increments. When there are no more checks, repeat with the other end. Then square both ends with a try square. Repeat the process for each board.

Interior finish work may require more than fresh end cuts. A damaged surface or an oversized board may have to be planed. To trim boards with accuracy, use a bench rule or a folding rule rather than a steel tape.

When you lay out cut lines on boards, always mark the angles—even if the angle is 90 degrees. All work on the job should be marked with a V to indicate a point, and a thin but

dark pencil line to indicate a cut. Bisect the V with the cut line. Then cut just outside this line, remembering to allow for the saw kerf. "Save the line" is the rule to remember when cutting. See illustration.

Right (90-degree) angles should be marked with a try square. All other angles should be calculated or transferred using either a steel protractor with a swing arm or a sliding bevel. A combination, or speed, square is good for marking 45-degree angles; a framing square can be used to mark any angle.

Marking a compound cut is a challenge. Start by determining the point that represents the farthest reach of the board. From this point mark both the side angle and the top angle. Set up the saw to follow both lines simultaneously. Experiment on scrap wood first.

Mortises, dowel holes, and other joint lines should be scribed with a marking gauge. This handy tool will also scribe accurate lines parallel to an edge for cutting strips or grooves. See illustration on page 26, left.

Measuring and Laying Out Panels

Many of the tools used to measure and lay out boards are also used for sheet paneling and wallboard. A steel tape is best for work on panels, however, because the edges are usually hidden, either by paneling trim or by wallboard tape and mud. Because moisture affects panels less than boards, they need not be squared. Trim the edges only if they are damaged, or if you need a smaller panel.

Using a Marking Gauge

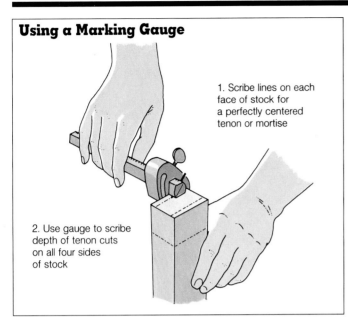

1. Scribe lines on each face of stock for a perfectly centered tenon or mortise

2. Use gauge to scribe depth of tenon cuts on all four sides of stock

Because you will usually be dealing with 4 by 8 sheets, it's advisable to use a framing square rather than a try square to mark right angles. If the floor-to-ceiling measurement for the first panel is 7 feet 8 inches, for example, don't automatically assume that the remaining such measurements will be too. Instead, measure for each panel as you progress around the room.

When marking cutouts use extra care. A mistake can ruin all or most of the panel. Use a bench rule if necessary and double-check the layout before you cut.

Marking a set of trammel points with a yardstick allows you to scribe circles up to 72 inches in diameter—large enough for most gable windows. See illustration at right. Irregular shapes can be transferred to the face of a panel with a compass. The metal point of the compass follows the irregular contour while the pencil marks the cut line. See illustration on page 76.

Setting Up Tools

Another aspect of measuring, too often overlooked, is the setting up of tools. Many tools used in carpentry have adjustable parts, such as blades, tables, and guides. Some even have built-in protractors and scales with which to set the movable pieces. These are fine for measuring angles on rough work, but don't trust them for finish carpentry. Instead, use a try square, a protractor, a sliding bevel, or a combination square to make sure that each angle is as it should be. See illustration.

When making and attaching jigs for use with hand or power tools, it is impossible to be too accurate. Extra care up front marks the true craftsman. The inaccuracies of a sloppy setup will be magnified as the job progresses. Use a bench rule, a caliper, a protractor, and a combination square for accurate setup work. Use scrap wood to test the jigs and setups and adjust as necessary before making the actual cut.

Using Trammel Points

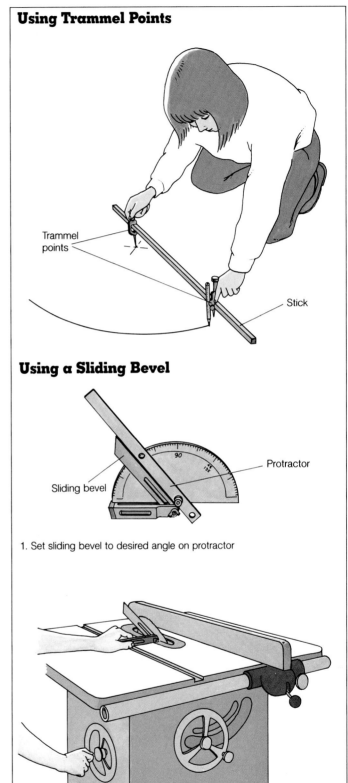

Trammel points

Stick

Using a Sliding Bevel

Sliding bevel

Protractor

1. Set sliding bevel to desired angle on protractor

2. Transfer this angle to saw blade

CUTTING

In recent years power tools, both portable and stationary, have proliferated. For jobs that are too small or too remote for a power tool, or for the person who enjoys working in the traditional manner, a wide selection of hand tools is also available. For clean, precise work, remember to keep sharp edges on all bits and blades.

The Simplest Cuts

Crosscuts—which run across the grain—and rip cuts—which run along it—are the two simplest kinds of cuts.

Crosscuts

These are the most basic cuts of all. A saw with 8 teeth per inch (TPI) is recommended for general crosscutting. Finer work, such as moldings, should be crosscut in a miter box using a 10- or 12-TPI blade. The portable circular saw and the stationary radial arm saw are particularly well suited for crosscutting boards, as is the power miter saw. These power saws are good for general cutting, used with a combination blade, but if you are going to do cutoffs or crosscuts exclusively, invest in a crosscut blade. A selection of cutting tools is shown in the photograph below.

Rip Cuts

Cutting a board lengthwise along the grain is called ripping. Hand ripsaws look nearly the same as hand crosscut saws, but the larger teeth are designed to chisel out bits of wood rather than slice it. Ripping can also be accomplished on a radial arm saw or a table saw, or with a circular saw. When ripping by hand, clamp a guide to the board—the grain of the wood can sometimes direct the blade off the cut line. The same type of guide should be used with a circular saw to ensure a straight cut. See illustration on page 28. The movable fence on a table saw ensures precise ripping.

To use a radial arm saw for ripping, turn it so that the blade is parallel to the back fence. Always feed the work into the blade, against the direction of rotation.

Angle Cuts

You can cut accurate angles on moldings with a miter box. If you are going to cut a lot of miters, or angle cuts, consider buying a power miter saw. This is a circular saw, hinged at the

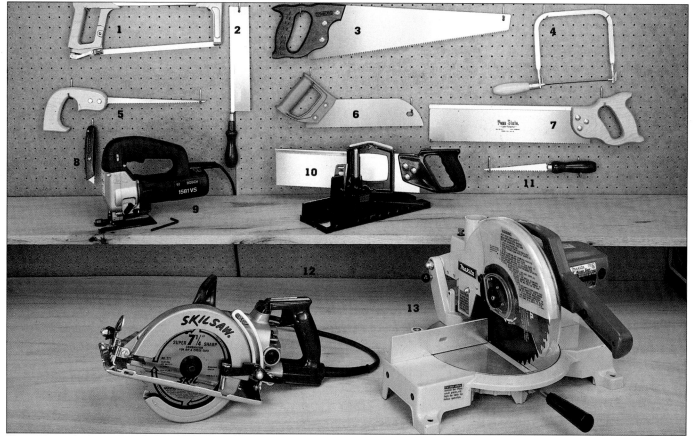

The cutting tools shown above include (1) hacksaw, (2) dovetail saw, (3) crosscut saw, (4) coping saw, (5) compass saw, (6) plywood saw, (7) tenon saw or backsaw, (8) utility knife, (9) saber saw, (10) miter box and saw, (11) wallboard saw, (12) circular saw, and (13) power miter saw.

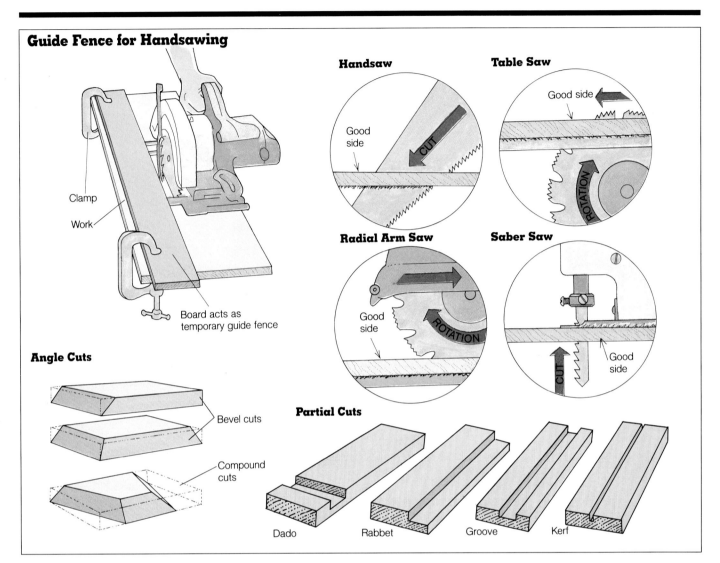

Guide Fence for Handsawing

Clamp

Work

Board acts as
temporary guide fence

Handsaw

Good
side

CUT

Table Saw

Good side

ROTATION

Radial Arm Saw

Good
side

ROTATION

Saber Saw

CUT

Good
side

Angle Cuts

Bevel cuts

Compound
cuts

Partial Cuts

Dado   Rabbet   Groove   Kerf

back, with a blade up to 14 inches in diameter (a 10-inch blade is the commonest). The pivoting saw motor is lowered onto the work, and the work is held against a fence.

For cutting along the length of a board or for making consistent square or other angle cuts, a table saw is best.

Power Miter Saw

This saw, illustrated opposite, can dramatically reduce the time and energy it takes to cut miters. Nearly as portable as the mechanical miter box and saw, the power miter saw

brings not only speed but also precision to the job. If first cuts need adjusting—you may be surprised at how many do—this saw is unbeatable.

The setup for a power miter saw is important. This tool operates at up to about 5,000 revolutions per minute (RPMs), so it's important to position it properly at the work station to prevent shifting. It's also important to support each end of the piece being cut by providing auxiliary worktables positioned at either end of the miter saw. This makes for

greater safety and for cleaner, more precise cuts. For maximum convenience the miter saw should be set up at waist height, with 6 feet of auxiliary support on each side. It's best to have a clear work space around this station; 15 feet on one end is usually sufficient.

A 10-inch power miter saw is adequate for most applications. This size is far more manageable than the larger models. A carbide-tipped blade is best for finish work.

When making cuts keep the saw table clean. Accumulated sawdust can cause work to misalign, and loose scrap can be

hurled forcefully in almost any direction.

It is best to experiment with this saw before plunging into the actual work, especially on angle cuts. Lay a piece of scrap wood flat on the saw table and notice where the cut begins. Then turn the wood on edge and repeat the process.

A word about safety: Resist the temptation to remove the guard when sawdust clings to it and obscures your view. Clean the guard, and leave it in place; it's there for a purpose. Someday it may save you from losing a finger.

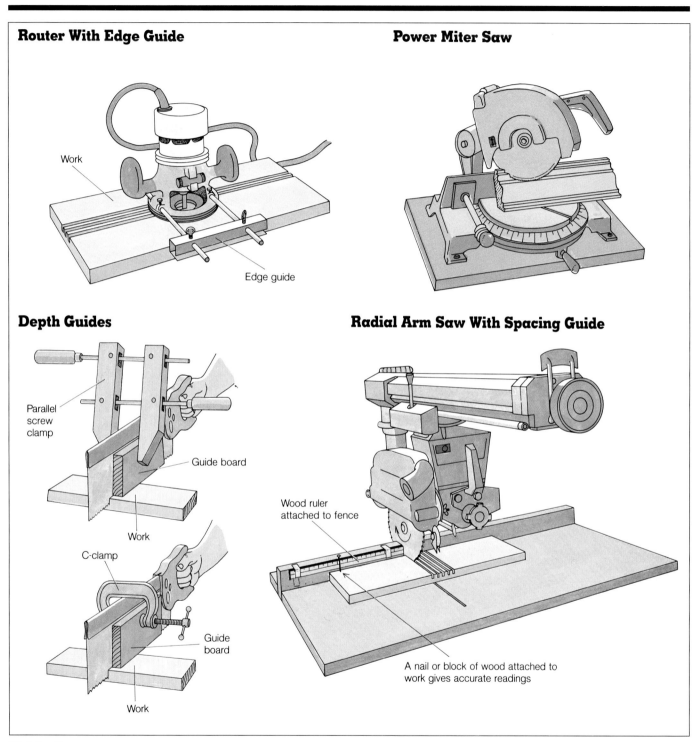

Router With Edge Guide

Work

Edge guide

Power Miter Saw

Depth Guides

Parallel screw clamp

Guide board

Work

C-clamp

Guide board

Work

Radial Arm Saw With Spacing Guide

Wood ruler attached to fence

A nail or block of wood attached to work gives accurate readings

Table Saw

Although all cutting can be done with a handsaw or a hand-held power saw, a table-mounted saw makes certain cuts more easily and swiftly.

With other types of saws, the saw blade moves through the work, which is held stationary. With the table saw the work is moved through the blade. For this reason your position relative to the table saw will be different from your position relative to other saws.

The table of the saw is usually large enough to support short pieces of stock as they're being cut. With longer stock auxiliary tables should be positioned for support.

A word of caution when using a table saw: To protect your eyes, always wear safety goggles. To protect your fingers, always know where they are relative to the blade. To move small pieces of stock past the blade, use a push stick—a suitably sized piece of wood (notched at the end, the better to hold the stock)—instead of your fingers.

To cut angles on boards and panels that, because of their size and shape, cannot be handled in a power miter saw or a table saw, clamp a guide to the work and then follow the guide with a handsaw or a circular saw. See illustration on page 28. A saber saw can be used on panels, but it tends to give a rough cut unless it is fitted with a special blade.

When cutting panels with a circular saw or a jigsaw, cut on the back. Since the blade cuts with an upward motion, the smoother side of the cut will be on the reverse, or finish, side of the board. When using a handsaw, a table saw, or a radial arm saw, cut with the face side up.

To make a bevel cut, position the work flat on the workbench or the saw table and tilt the blade. Any type of saw that makes a crosscut or a rip cut can also be used to make a bevel cut. With a power saw follow the directions for tilting the blade or the table.

A cut that combines an angle and a bevel is called a compound cut. The hardest part of executing a compound cut is calculating it and marking the cut line. Once that is done, setting up the saw poses no problem. A radial arm saw and a table saw with a miter gauge are both especially good for making compound cuts, because they can be adjusted in two directions.

Partial Cuts

You will sometimes need to make cuts that go only partway through the board. They include rabbets, dadoes, grooves, and kerfs. See illustration on page 28.

By hand these cuts are made with a backsaw—a handsaw with a metal rib along the back. Clamp a piece of wood to the blade to act as a depth guide. See illustration on page 29. Since a handsaw has a narrow kerf, you'll have to make several parallel cuts and then chisel out the center portion to make a wide groove.

Both a table saw and a radial arm saw can be fitted with dado blades. Some of these blades have a fixed width; others are adjustable. All are designed to create a wide dado, or groove, in one pass. If you need to make repeated cuts in a single piece of wood, fasten a wood ruler to the fence of the saw. A nail, or a block of wood fastened to the end of the board, will enable you to sight your measurement more accurately.

The router is designed specifically for making partial cuts. A hand router isn't often used, but a power router is a valuable tool. A wide selection of router bits and accessories is available. Two accessories very useful for making partial cuts are the edge guide and the router table. Set the guide or adjust the fence to produce a straight cut or a series of parallel cuts.

Use carbide bits in your router; they will last longer and produce smoother work than other bits. To prevent the bit from breaking and from burning or chipping the stock, try not to cut more than ⅜ inch deep in a single pass. Be careful to feed the work into the router at a moderate, even speed. If fine dust rather than sawdust is being produced, you're feeding the work too slowly, which can cause the bit to heat up and burn the stock. If large curls of waste are being produced and you hear the RPMs drop dramatically, you're feeding the work too fast.

To get a board to bend without breaking, saw a series of parallel kerfs on the back. Because a great many small cuts are necessary, a power saw, such as a radial arm saw, is more efficient than a handsaw. Experiment with extra stock to determine how deep the kerfs must be and how they must be spaced to produce the flexibility you desire.

Curved Cuts

To install a lock it is necessary to cut one or more holes in the door. Originally this was done with a keyhole saw or a compass saw. Nowadays it's done much faster with a hole saw—an attachment for an electric drill that has a pilot drill in the center surrounded by a serrated ring. Interchangeable saw blades are available in a wide variety of sizes.

To cut large circles and irregular shapes, follow a pencil line with a compass saw or a keyhole saw. For smaller shapes use a coping saw.

In all cases, sawing will be neater and more efficient if you provide support for the work. As you cut, continue to reposition the piece on sawhorses or on the workbench to keep the piece from vibrating. If you are cutting several pieces to the same length, clamp or nail them together, then make a single cut.

The band saw, jigsaw, and saber saw are all designed to make circular and irregular cuts. The relatively narrow depth of the blade on these saws allows it to follow curves without binding. Some saber saws come with a combination edge guide and circle cutter attached. The circle cutter—an arm with a pin on the bottom—allows you to pivot the saw around a center point.

Joints in Wood

Some wood joints are so famous that they have saws named after them—or maybe it's the other way around. In any case, the complete woodworker's toolbox includes a tenon saw, a dovetail saw, and a coping saw.

Joints in Wood

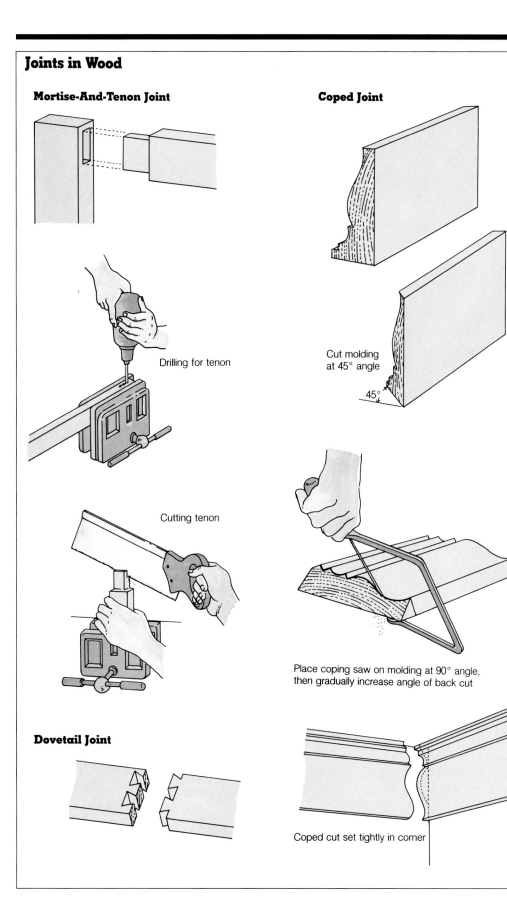

Mortise-And-Tenon Joint

Drilling for tenon

Cutting tenon

Coped Joint

Cut molding at 45° angle

45°

Place coping saw on molding at 90° angle, then gradually increase angle of back cut

Coped cut set tightly in corner

Dovetail Joint

Mortise-And-Tenon Joint

Unlike the lap joint or the coped joint, the mortise-and-tenon joint requires that both of the boards to be joined be cut. See illustration. The tenon is formed on one board by marking and sawing away blocks. The tenon saw gives precise control for straight cuts, but unless you have a good eye and a steady hand, clamp a depth guide block to the blade before making the tenon cuts. Do the four end cuts first and then the four side cuts.

The radial arm saw and the table saw do a fine job of cutting tenons. Set the depth of the cut as required and make several passes to remove all the material. Use this same method to cut tenons with a band saw or a jigsaw.

Every tenon needs a mortise. One of the two ways to cut a mortise is to mark the board accurately and then carve out the recess with a chisel the same size as the mortise you are cutting. The other method is to use a mortising bit installed in a drill press or a mortising apparatus. This bit drills a round hole, which the square housing chisels into a rectangle. Unless your tenon is exactly square, you will have to make several cuts with the mortising bit.

Dovetail Joint

When done well by hand, the dovetail joint is a work of art. To execute it takes skill and patience—and a dovetail saw. Careful marking is more than half the battle.

The band saw and jigsaw can also be used to execute

dovetails, but the same careful measuring is called for. A sure-fire way to make perfect dovetail joints is to use a router, a dovetail bit, and a dovetail jig. Secure both boards in the jig, one positioned horizontally and the other vertically, and cut them at the same time. The sign of a routed dovetail joint is that only one side shows evidence of the cuts.

Coped Joint

This joint, which requires that only one piece be cut, is best executed with a coping saw. See illustration on page 31. For the tightest fit when cutting molding, for example, start the coping cut at a 90-degree angle to the back of the workpiece. This initial top cut will show as a final part of the joint. Direct the rest of the cut slightly inward, away from the molding to be joined. This will ensure good contact between the two pieces of molding at the visible edges. To avoid vibration while working on thin stock and to create a clean cut, support the stock close to the cut.

Working With Veneer

As hardwood increases in price, veneer becomes more popular. Improved adhesives and tools make working with veneers easier than ever. For the traditional woodworker, glue pots and hide glue are still available; the latter is mixed with water, heated, and painted on with a brush. However, white polyvinyl resin glue is so universally used these days that it comes in 55-gallon drums as well as the standard squeeze bottle.

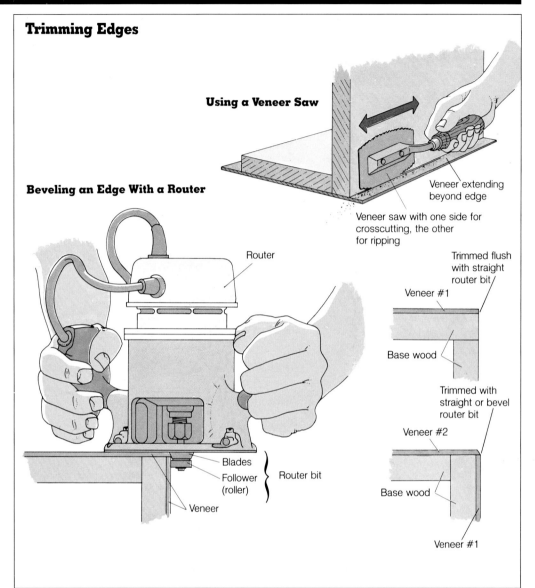

Trimming Edges

Using a Veneer Saw

Veneer extending beyond edge

Veneer saw with one side for crosscutting, the other for ripping

Beveling an Edge With a Router

Router

Blades
Follower (roller)
} Router bit

Veneer

Trimmed flush with straight router bit

Veneer #1

Base wood

Trimmed with straight or bevel router bit

Veneer #2

Base wood

Veneer #1

Large areas of veneer should be clamped while the glue dries. Transverse boards clamped along the edges will ensure good adhesion. If you use contact cement on veneer, you need not clamp the work. Paint the glue onto the surfaces to be bonded, let it dry (set up), position the pieces carefully, and press them together. When they touch they bond and cannot be moved. If you need to break the bond, there is only one way. Dribble a small amount of lacquer thinner into the joint and pull the pieces apart gently, applying more thinner as you go. A plastic squeeze bottle with a small opening works well. When the pieces are separated, let them dry until tacky, reposition them, and press them back together. It is usually not necessary to reglue them.

Once the glue has set up, the edges can be trimmed. A veneer saw made for this purpose has a side-mounted handle, and the cutting teeth are flush on one side to prevent you from overcutting the edge. This saw is inexpensive, compact, and well suited to small jobs. See illustration. To trim long lengths use an electric router. A special laminate trimmer blade has a roller to follow the surface of the work. At a corner use the chamfered trimmer to put a slight bevel on one edge. This bevel makes the veneer or laminate less prone to chipping. A file can also be used to bevel edges.

SHAPING

Unlike the cuts already discussed, shaping involves the cutting away of wood for decorative reasons—to create moldings and molded edges. Although much of the shaped wood used in today's homes is produced in lumber mills, you can extend the variety and even duplicate antique moldings by making your own.

Moldings and Molded Edges

The tools used in making moldings are specialized, but they are readily available to the amateur woodworker. A selection is shown in the photograph at right. In addition, some basic power tools, such as the table saw, the radial arm saw, and the router, can be used for shaping.

Virtually all of today's moldings have a linear design: The relief runs across the grain and the dimensions are constant along the grain. This means that the carpenter must feed the boards lengthwise past the shaper bit no matter what tool the bit is attached to. The bit, or combination of bits, that you affix to the spindle determines the final shape of the molding.

Adjust the fence so that the cutting portion of the shaper bit protrudes. Hold the work firmly against the table and fence as you slide it past the bit. Be sure to feed the work against the rotation of the bit to avoid the danger of kickback.

Cutting a design across the end of a board requires a different setup. The board will probably be too narrow to slide along the fence. Leave the fence in position, but use the miter gauge and slot on the tabletop to hold the board. Move it on a steady path across the cutter, keeping it perpendicular to the fence. See illustration on page 107. When edging all four sides of a board, do the ends first and then the long sides.

Surface Patterns

Occasionally you will want to cut a molded pattern along the face of a board. Use a router, a table saw, or a radial arm saw. To use a router, clamp a guide board onto the work and move the router along it. See illustration on page 34. Cutting flutes is done in this way; by using different bits or by making several passes, you can create many different effects.

To create a panel or plaque with a continuous design, make a template containing the pattern for one side and a corner. Attach this to the work and follow the pattern with the router. When you have completed the cut, remount the template. This way all sides and corners will be identical.

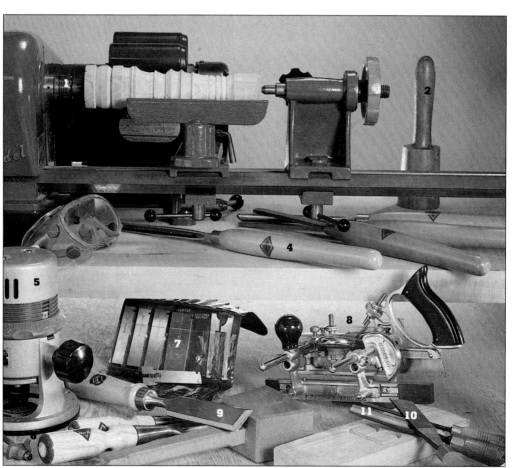

The shaping tools shown above include (1) bench lathe, (2) wooden mallet, (3) safety goggles, (4) wood-turning tools, (5) portable power router, (6) router bits, (7) multiplane cutters, (8) multiplane, (9) chisel, (10) skew, and (11) gouge.

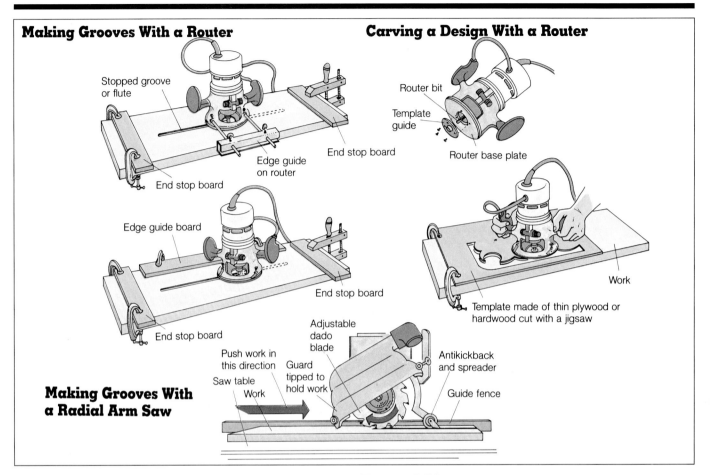

Making Grooves With a Router

Stopped groove or flute

Edge guide on router

End stop board

End stop board

Edge guide board

End stop board

End stop board

Making Grooves With a Radial Arm Saw

Carving a Design With a Router

Router bit

Template guide

Router base plate

End stop board

Work

Template made of thin plywood or hardwood cut with a jigsaw

Adjustable dado blade

Push work in this direction

Guard tipped to hold work

Saw table

Work

Antikickback and spreader

Guide fence

Using the table saw for surface cuts is simple—just crank the molding head to the desired height, lock the fence in position, and feed the material through. The bits tend to lift the material as it passes over, so exert a little pressure near the head (use a push stick if necessary), or attach a pressure arm jig to the fence.

To use the radial arm saw for surface cuts, rotate the saw 90 degrees so that the blade is parallel to the fence. Then feed the work through against the rotation of the blade. See illustration.

The router is by far the best power tool to use for freehand designs, such as numbers or letters, recessed into the surface of a board. After accurately penciling the design onto the board, follow the shapes carefully with the router as far as the radius of the bit will allow. Use a chisel to clean out and square up the corners.

For a small design it may be easier to work by hand, using chisels and a mallet, or gouges. You can even execute straight surface designs and borders by hand with a hand router or a multiplane. These tools operate in the same way as a hand plane, but they are fitted with variously shaped cutting blades and adjustable fences, so that designs can be cut parallel to the edges of a board. These traditional tools may be hard to find in retail stores, but they are available through mail-order catalogs.

Turned Pieces

Balusters, newel posts, and drawer knobs can be turned on a lathe. Producing these items would not justify the cost of even a used lathe, but if you'd also like to make chair or table legs, bowls, or candlesticks, you'll need this tool.

To make balusters you'll need a lathe with a capacity of 36 inches or more. You'll also need a basic selection of turning tools, including ¼-inch, ½-inch, and ¾-inch gouges; a ¾-inch round-nosed scraper; a 1-inch skew chisel; and a ¼-inch V-parting tool.

Select clear stock with no checks, cracks, or splits. Locate the center on each end by drawing intersecting lines at 90 degrees to each other. Mark the centers with a hole punch. Mount the stock in the lathe and adjust the tool rest so that it is ⅛ inch above the centerline and ⅛ inch away from the wood. With the lathe at slow speed (approximately 800 RPMs), start shaping the work by easing the edge of a chisel or gouge into the wood. Hold the tool firmly and work from the center toward each end. Next, increase the speed appropriate to the hardness of the wood and finish the work with the appropriate wood-turning tools, using a caliper to transfer the dimensions from the master drawing to the workpiece. Finally, smooth the surface of the work with strips of sandpaper—first medium, then fine.

 URFACING

To achieve the smoothest surfaces, it is generally better to surface each component before it is installed. Indeed, some pieces must be surfaced in order to fit. Others must be surfaced to eliminate saw cut marks, raised grain resulting from exposure to moisture, and damage suffered during transport. Smooth surfaces also result in neater and much stronger joints.

Rules and Tools

To achieve consistently good results, follow two basic rules: Always use sharp tools. Study the grain of the wood and work the surface accordingly.

You will need a variety of tools and materials: hand and power planes, a jointer, files, rasps, a Surform® plane, sandpaper, and scrapers. A selection of surfacing tools is shown in the photograph below. For surfaces that need filling or building up rather than planing down, add wood putty and liquid sealer-fillers to the list.

The tools, materials, and techniques (including surfacing) used in working with wallboard are described on pages 67 to 74. Refer to these pages for specifics. The following discussion covers working with wood.

Maintaining a Keen Cutting Edge

Always use sharp tools. Tools with metal edges should be sharpened on a whetstone. If the blade is very dull or mis-shapen, dress it first on a grinding wheel, being careful to maintain the original beveled angle. See illustration on page 36, top. Move the blade back and forth across the wheel using light pressure. Don't press hard enough to generate heat, or the temper of the edge will be lost.

A two-sided whetstone is used for sharpening and then honing the edge after grinding. Increase the original angle of bevel slightly as you hone.

With normal use tungsten carbide blades will outlast high-speed steel ones; therefore these more expensive blades are more economical in the long run.

The surfacing tools shown above include (1) wood-body smoothing plane, (2) metal-body jack plane, (3) sanding belts, (4) sanding accessories for drills, (5) orbital finishing sander, (6) sanding block and sandpaper, (7) portable power planer, (8) block plane, (9) spokeshave, (10) scraper plates, (11) Surform® plane, (12) assorted rasps and file, (13) triangular files and rifflers, and (14) two-sided rasp.

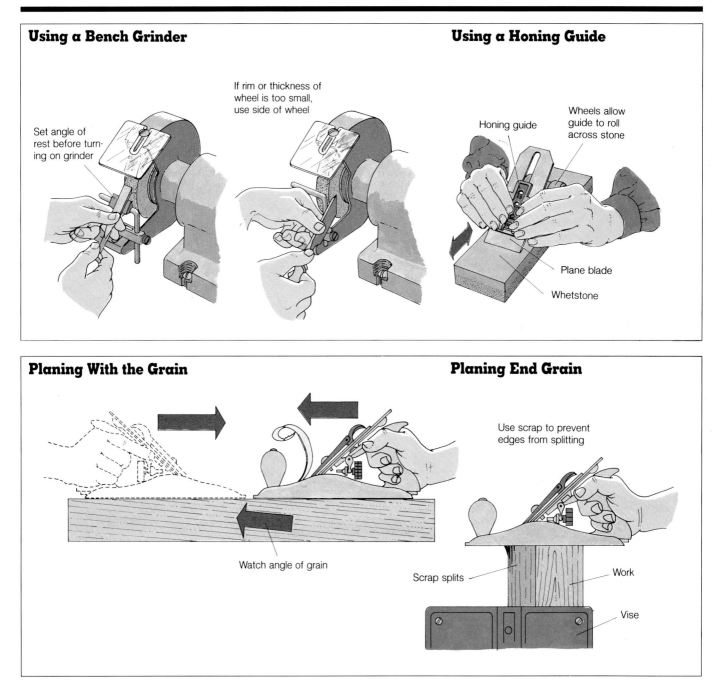

Using a Bench Grinder

Set angle of rest before turning on grinder

If rim or thickness of wheel is too small, use side of wheel

Using a Honing Guide

Honing guide

Wheels allow guide to roll across stone

Plane blade

Whetstone

Planing With the Grain

Watch angle of grain

Planing End Grain

Use scrap to prevent edges from splitting

Scrap splits

Work

Vise

Working With the Grain

Reading wood grain is simply a matter of observing whether it runs lengthwise or crosswise. Except when working with the end grain, all surfacing is done lengthwise. Before surfacing the face or side of a board, observe the direction of the grain. Then take a closer look to determine which way is uphill. See bottom illustration (above). Although boards with a grain pattern perfectly parallel to the surface can be worked either way, most boards are best worked in the uphill direction.

This allows the cutting or scraping tool to cut the wood fibers rather than break them. The result is an easier job and a smoother surface.

The end of the board can be smoothed in either direction, since the end grain is nondirectional. Use sharp tools to avoid compressing the wood fibers and opening spaces between them; this makes the surface rough and porous. It is also important when working with end grain to avoid splitting. Clamp a piece of scrap wood to the edge of the work and let that piece split instead, or make a small bevel (called a chamfer) along the edge. The

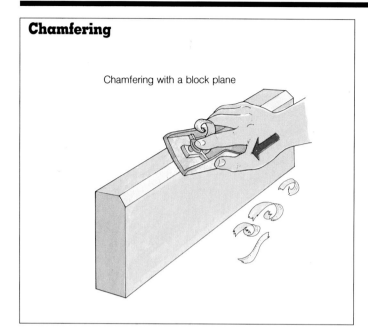

Chamfering

Chamfering with a block plane

chamfer method is best, provided you can smooth the bevel later by trimming or surfacing the length of the board. A third method is to work from each edge toward the center of the piece. It is difficult to get a really square surface by this method, but it does prevent splitting.

Planes

To surface wood by hand, you need a jack plane, a smoothing plane, and a block plane. All three are available with wood or metal bodies, and all have similar cutting irons. Use the jack plane when working rough timber down to size or when removing large amounts of wood from a straight board. The 14-inch to 17-inch sole-plate bridges depressions and takes off only the high spots—good for initial cuts when you are actually establishing a level. Follow up with the smoothing plane, which has an 8-inch to 10-inch soleplate. The curl produced by this plane marks your

progress. When you produce a smooth, thin curl, the piece is sufficiently planed.

A block plane is more compact than the other types, and it is light enough to control with one hand. Use it to plane end grains and put chamfers on large boards. See illustration.

A small power plane can be used in place of these three hand planes. A power plane makes quick work of edge-planing jobs, and it can also be used for surface planing.

Jointers

Hand planing is laborious and time-consuming, even for small jobs. The jointer—essentially a mechanized stationary plane— saves a lot of time and energy, and it turns out work that is smooth and square. Select a jointer capable of handling

a board at least 4 inches wide. You'll find even more uses for a model that will handle a 6-inch or 8-inch board.

Before turning on the machine, observe which way the blades travel as they cut away the wood. Position the workpiece so that the wood is cut in the uphill direction. Always feed the work against the rotation of the blades. To avoid chipping the end of a board, first make a small (½-inch to 1-inch) false start with the work reversed. Then back the work up, turn it around, and make the main pass. Never tamper with the guard on the jointer.

To plane the edges of boards on the jointer, construct a wooden fence out of ¾-inch plywood. Make it 12 inches high and attach it to the regular fence. The added height eliminates wobbling when you feed boards through in an upright position.

Files and Rasps

Curved shapes in wood are usually cut with a band saw, a jigsaw, a saber saw, or any of the handsaws capable of cutting a radius. Irregular shapes and reliefs are sometimes chiseled or gouged out by hand. All of these methods leave a surface made up of small irregular cuts that must be smoothed out. Wood files, rasps, and the Surform® plane are the tools used for this purpose.

Files with single-cut teeth (that is, teeth that cut in one direction) will produce a smoother surface than double-cut files. Rasps and double-cut files, however, are less prone to clogging than single-cut files. Files and rasps are available in four grades—coarse, bastard,

second, and smooth. A four-in-hand rasp combines all four on the slightly rounded surfaces of a single tool. Some carpenters prefer the finer metal files for smoothing wood, even though they clog more easily.

The Surform® plane is related to both the hand plane and the rasp. Its blade is stamped out of sheet metal and then ground in such a way that the surface is covered with small cutting edges. The plane is available with a variety of handles that are designed to hold blades of different shapes. The blades should be replaced when they become dull.

The key to success when using files (or any other smoothing tool) is to keep the wood from chattering, or vibrating, as you work. Secure the piece with a vise or clamp; use side supports if it is thin. If the wood chips or splinters when you work the end grain, clamp a bit of scrap against (and level with) the splintering edge. Always make sure that your files are sharp.

Rifflers are small files or rasps. They come in a great variety of sizes and shapes. Use them to smooth the hard-to-reach areas created in wood carving. They are also useful for cleaning out the small rounded corners left by the router bit. Small curved and irregular areas can also be smoothed with any one of several attachments to an electric drill, including rotary files, rotary rasps, and even a drum type of Surform® tool.

Sanders and Scrapers

Say "surfacing" and most people think immediately of sandpaper. Nearly every piece of finished wood has been smoothed by this useful material at some point. Each sandpaper has its own grading system; refer to the chart on page 18.

When you sand by hand, always use a block to back up the paper. With inside curves wrap the paper around a bit of dowel or closet pole, or make a sanding block out of the scrap piece from the cut.

Several power sanding machines are available to the do-it-yourselfer. The stationary disk sander and the belt sander are ideal for large projects. Among the hand-held models, the belt sander is capable of surfacing large areas quickly. For small areas the orbital sander is less expensive and more portable. Perhaps its greatest virtue is that it uses partial sheets of regular sandpaper, which are quickly and easily changed. Sanding attachments can be used to convert a table saw, a radial arm saw, and an electric drill motor to a disk sander.

For smoothing flat surfaces a scraper plate can be used in place of sandpaper. The edges of this 4-inch by 5-inch metal sheet can be renewed periodically by filing and burnishing. Use a scraping motion to produce a smooth, flat surface. See illustration. The plate is inexpensive, and it will outlast hundreds of sheets of sandpaper. Curved plates are also available in a variety of shapes and sizes for use on irregular surfaces. Remember to scrape or sand in the direction of the grain of the wood.

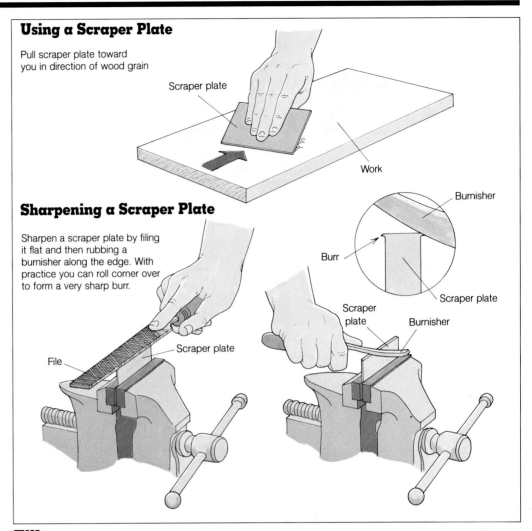

Using a Scraper Plate

Pull scraper plate toward you in direction of wood grain

Scraper plate

Work

Sharpening a Scraper Plate

Sharpen a scraper plate by filing it flat and then rubbing a burnisher along the edge. With practice you can roll corner over to form a very sharp burr.

File

Scraper plate

Scraper plate

Burnisher

Burr

Scraper plate

Scraper plate

Burnisher

Fillers

To hide small gaps in finish work, or to fill the depressions left when the finishing nails were set, use wood putty. Apply it in small amounts and sand it smooth when it is dry. Choose a color that matches the color of the natural wood. When it dries it will stain and finish like the natural wood.

Several open-grained woods are used in finish carpentry; they include oak, mahogany, walnut, and chestnut. These woods have large, open pores, which must be filled before sealing to produce a smooth surface. Use a paste wood filler thinned down to the consistency of syrup, or thin according to the manufacturer's instructions. Choose a color to match the unfinished wood. Paint on the filler with a stiff brush, working it well into the open pores. When the filler is nearly dry (when it balls up on your thumb as you rub it), remove the excess with a loosely folded or crumpled rag. Wipe across the grain to avoid pulling the filler out of the pores.

After you have removed most of the filler, let the work dry overnight. The next day lightly sand the surface, in the direction of the grain. You are now ready to apply the finish.

Caution: Rags used to apply or remove wood-finishing substances should be hung loosely in a ventilated area, stored underwater, or disposed of immediately. Spontaneous combustion may occur if rags are crumpled, stacked, or stored in a closed area.

FASTENING

Nails, screws, glue, and dowels are the most commonly used fastenings. Logic will usually dictate the correct choice. Examples of various types of fastenings are shown in the illustration on page 40.

Nailing

Many kinds of nails have been designed to meet the fastening requirements of various materials. In addition, corrugated fasteners and wood joiners are commonly used (along with glue) to secure mitered corners. Like nails, these fasteners are driven in with a hammer. Use the illustration on page 40 as a guide to selecting the right nail for the job.

Hammers

If you are buying just one hammer, choose a 16-ounce curved claw. It will be adequate for most finish carpentry work. The bell face will help you to avoid creating quarter moons as you drive nails home, and the claw will remove small and medium-sized nails. When pulling nails from any finish work, put a thin piece of scrap under the hammerhead to protect the surface.

If you are installing wood shakes or shingles to the roof or sides of a house, use a shingling hatchet; it has a slightly curved, checked face for driving nails. For lighter nailing a 5-ounce to 8-ounce tack hammer or Warrington hammer is better than the full-sized curved claw. These smaller hammers let you start brads, tacks, and nails without hitting your fingers, and they are easier to control in tight areas and around glazed windows.

Occasionally you will need a really heavy hammer. A 20-ounce to 28-ounce ripping hammer may do for tightening up tongue-and-groove flooring or driving a peg or a large stake, but the job will probably be easier with a 5-pound short-handled sledge or dead-blow hammer. Older dead-blow hammers have heads of solid lead. The faces deform easily and are not intended for nailing, but the hammers deliver a tremendous blow. Some newer models have a plastic casting filled with lead shot. A variety of hammers is shown in the photograph at left.

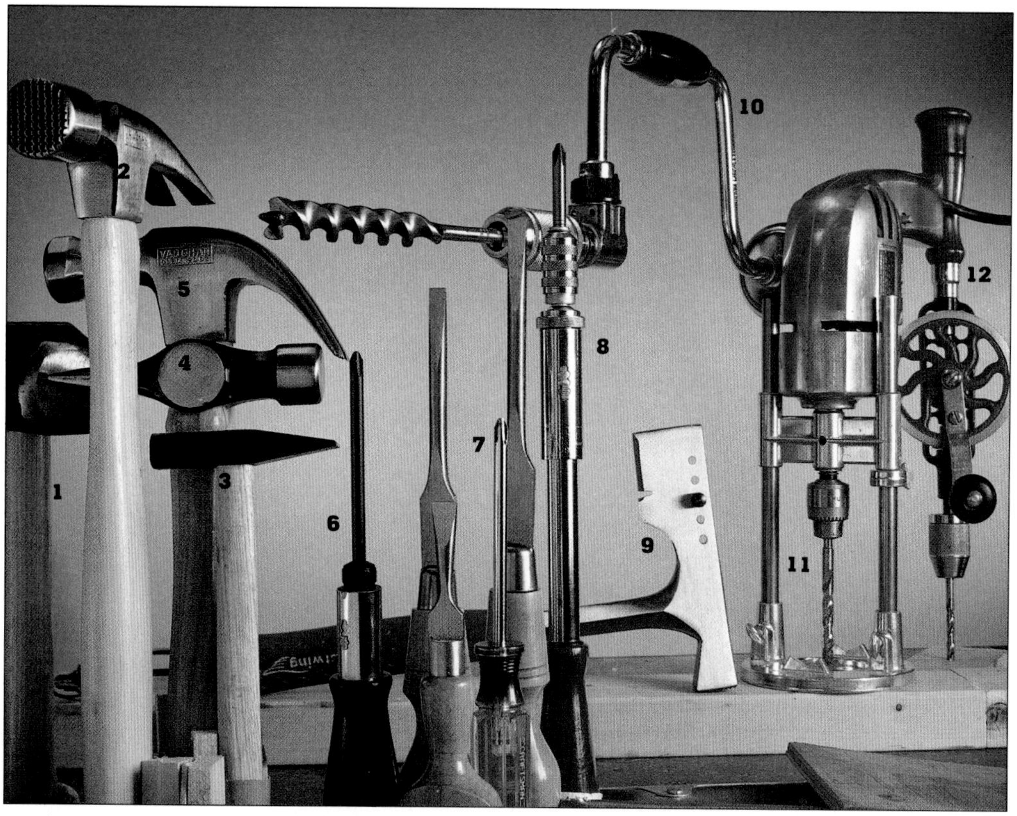

Helpful Hints

To maximize the holding power of nails along a single piece of wood, angle them in alternate directions as you drive them in. The board will be less likely to work loose as it dries out or as the weight load shifts. See illustration on page 41.

To prevent boards from splitting when nailed near the ends, nail at an angle against the grain, or through the annual rings, not between them. If you can't see which way the annual rings run, blunt the nail before driving it. This will cause the nail to shear the wood fibers as it passes through them, an effect somewhat similar to that caused by drilling a hole. Drilling a hole, in fact, is the surest way to avoid splitting. Make pilot holes approximately two thirds of the diameter of the nail shank.

The fastening tools shown above include (1) four-pound sledgehammer, (2) checkered-face ripping hammer, (3) brad hammer, (4) Warrington hammer, (5) claw hammer, (6) ratchet screwdriver with Phillips-head bit, (7) assorted screwdrivers with slotted-head bits, (8) Yankee screwdriver, (9) shingling hatchet, (10) brace and auger bit, (11) portable drill with guide, and (12) hand drill.

Nails

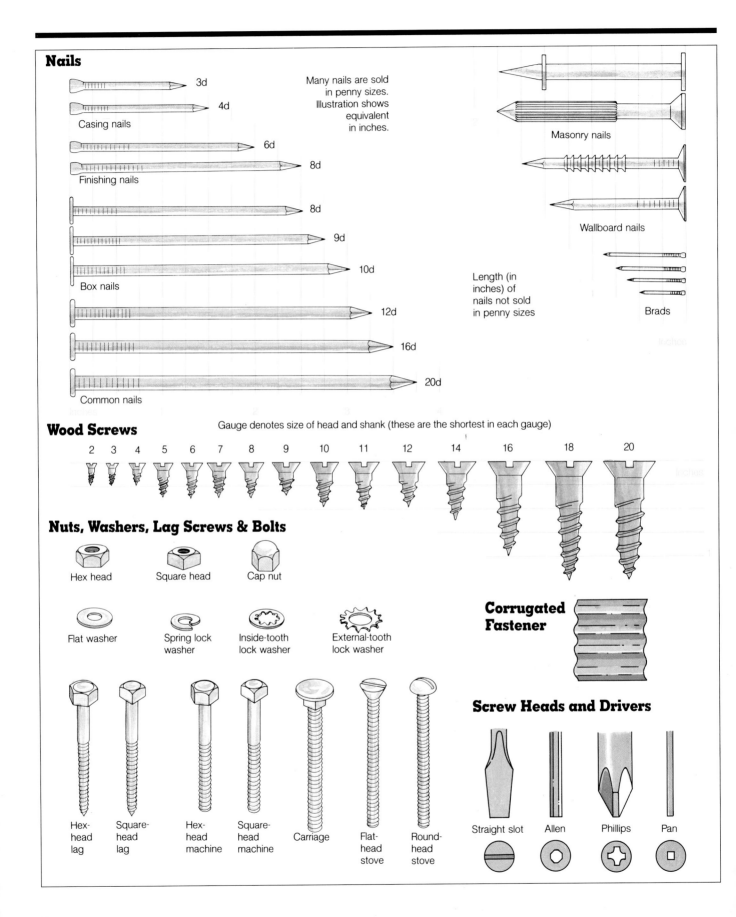

3d
4d
Casing nails

6d
8d
Finishing nails

8d
9d
10d
Box nails

12d
16d
20d
Common nails

Many nails are sold
in penny sizes.
Illustration shows
equivalent
in inches.

Masonry nails

Wallboard nails

Length (in
inches) of
nails not sold
in penny sizes

Brads

Wood Screws

Gauge denotes size of head and shank (these are the shortest in each gauge)

2   3   4   5   6   7   8   9   10   11   12   14   16   18   20

Nuts, Washers, Lag Screws & Bolts

Hex head   Square head   Cap nut

Flat washer   Spring lock   Inside-tooth   External-tooth
                  washer   lock washer   lock washer

Hex-   Square-   Hex-   Square-   Carriage   Flat-   Round-
head   head   head   head   head   head
lag   lag   machine   machine   stove   stove

Corrugated Fastener

Screw Heads and Drivers

Straight slot   Allen   Phillips   Pan

40

Nailing

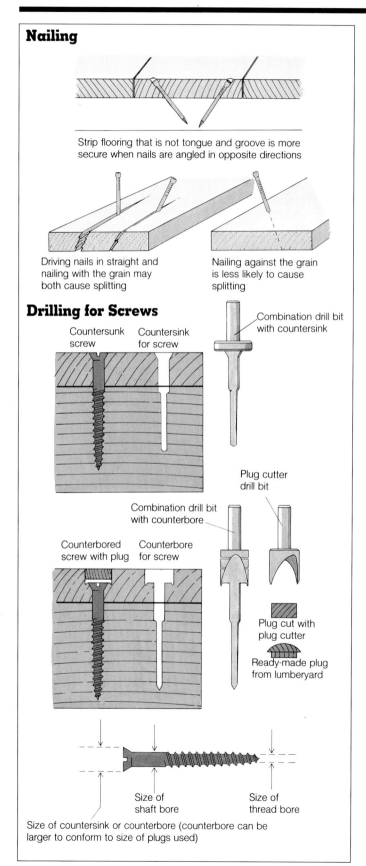

Strip flooring that is not tongue and groove is more secure when nails are angled in opposite directions

Driving nails in straight and nailing with the grain may both cause splitting

Nailing against the grain is less likely to cause splitting

Drilling for Screws

Countersunk screw   Countersink for screw

Combination drill bit with countersink

Plug cutter drill bit

Combination drill bit with counterbore

Counterbored screw with plug   Counterbore for screw

Plug cut with plug cutter

Ready-made plug from lumberyard

Size of shaft bore   Size of thread bore

Size of countersink or counterbore (counterbore can be larger to conform to size of plugs used)

Pneumatic Nailers, Staplers, and Nailing Guns

A pneumatic nailer is a great help to the carpenter faced with a large project. It can be used for nailing exterior and interior trim. A pneumatic stapler is handy when the fastening will not be visible, such as for sheathing, subflooring, and roofing. A power-actuated nailing gun, which is used to attach sleepers or furring strips to concrete, takes .22-caliber cartridges and special nails. It is potentially very dangerous and must be used with extreme caution. In some areas only licensed contractors may buy or rent this tool.

As with the selection of any tool, the proper choice of a pneumatic tool will make a big difference in the results achieved. First, ask yourself whether the size and complexity of the job warrant spending the money to buy a pneumatic tool, a compressor, and the required accessories. If not, does the job warrant renting this equipment? Should the answer to either question be yes, the following information is for you. The discussion focuses on pneumatic nailers, since they are usually the most appropriate pneumatic tool for the fastening required in finish carpentry.

Pneumatic nailers have a two-step firing sequence in order to meet safety requirements. To drive a nail you must depress the shoe, or work-contacting element, against the work as you pull the trigger. This feature prevents the nailer from firing like a gun—activated by the trigger only.

The best firing sequence for finish work is called the sequential trip, or trip-then-trigger. You must fully release the trigger before you can drive the next nail. This scheme allows for more accurate positioning of the nailer and a better nailing pattern than the firing sequence known as bounce nailing, or the contact trip. The sequential trip is also safer, because the nailer will not fire with accidental contact while the trigger is being held.

It's important to select the right nail, of the right length, for the job. For most exterior finish work, choose a nail that will penetrate beyond the material to be fastened by a ratio of about 2 to 1. That is, if the material to be fastened is ¾ inch thick, the nail should be about 1½ inches longer than that thickness, or 2¼ inches overall. More penetration is generally better than less, so a slightly longer nail is acceptable. For exterior finish work select a nail with a galvanized finish. Better yet is a stainless steel nail, but be prepared to pay a premium. For interior finish work, smooth nails are standard (and the most economical).

Many brands and models of pneumatic nailer can accommodate nails in the range of lengths mentioned above. Some have nail magazines that extend at right angles to the nail-driving mechanism; others have angled magazines, which allow for a little more maneuverability. Give some thought to the various nailing positions that will be required of any nailer; this will help you to select the right tool.

Once the nailer is on the job site, take some time to practice before you start nailing. Drive several nails into a scrap of the material you'll be working on, using some suitable backing. You'll get a feel for the nailer and a chance to observe the effect of the nail head on the wood. It is usually best to drive the nail so that the head winds up parallel to the grain (in most cases, parallel to the length of the workpiece). If the nailer can be set to allow the nail to be driven to various depths, experiment to get the depth you want. Practice until you are satisfied with the results.

If you're buying a pneumatic tool, investigate the capabilities of different models before making a final decision. If you're renting, talk to several rental stores about their equipment, in order to get the most suitable tool for your project. Whether buying or renting, insist on a demonstration and some instruction to make sure that you get the best tool for the job.

Nearly as important as the selection of the tool is the choice of the compressor and hoses. Compressors come in different sizes and shapes and with different capabilities. Tank size for portable compressors for finish nailers, for example, ranges from 1 to 4 gallons. As for hoses, the better the quality, the more consistent the inner diameter of the hose and the smoother the action of the nailer.

Safety is important when you work with pneumatic tools. Wear safety goggles, as you would when operating any power tool. Study the owner's manual. Understand what you are doing before you begin.

Screwing

Screws are stronger fasteners than nails, although they are more expensive and take longer to install. Drill pilot holes for fastening wood to wood. This makes the screw easier to seat and also creates a stronger bond.

Boring for Screws

A time-consuming but necessary preparatory task is boring pilot holes for screws. See illustration on page 41 for an example of a tapered counterbore for a plugged flat-head wood screw. Drilling this type of bore is much easier and faster with a combination bit—either with a countersink or a counterbore. The bits come in configurations matching particular screw sizes. The former will drill a tapered hole for a countersunk screw. The latter will drill a tapered hole for a counterbored screw and plug in one operation.

You can prepare a pilot hole without a combination bit, but you will have to use two drill bits and either a countersink or a counterbore bit. To drill a pilot hole for a countersunk screw, bore the hole for the shank first, making it equal to the shank diameter. Next, bore the hole for the threaded portion of the screw. The diameter of the hole should equal the diameter of the shaft (threads excluded). Then use the countersink bit. The countersink for a flat-head screw should be equal, at its widest point, to the diameter of the screw head. To drill the pilot hole for a counterbored screw, use the counterbore bit first, then bore the hole for the shank and the

threaded portion of the screw, as described above.

Driving Screws

To drive slotted screws, use a conventional flat-blade screwdriver. Keep the edges sharp and square, to avoid slipping and burring the slot. Choose the correct size of screwdriver so that you do not deform either the tool or the screw head. When driving Phillips-head screws, make sure that the screwdriver fits snugly into and reaches to the bottom of the slots.

Because the pan-head screw is much easier to drive than either of the other types of screws, it is gaining in popularity. It has a square hole and is driven by a square-headed bit. The head is much smaller than other screw heads and can be countersunk without predrilling.

Ratchet screwdrivers with interchangeable bits, including the push-driven (or Yankee) version, are a great time-saver. Special bits are available to convert ¼-inch and ⅜-inch ratchet

(wrench) drivers to either Phillips or flat-blade screwdrivers. A hand brace can also be fitted with screwdriver bits.

Power Screwdriving

Regular ¼-inch and ⅜-inch drill motors accommodate special screwdriver bits with hexagonal shafts, but make sure that the drill has a slow or continuously variable speed. If you are buying a drill with screwdriving in mind, choose one with reversible speed.

An alternative to nailing wallboard to joints and studs is to attach it with wallboard screws, using a special drill (see illustration on page 69, bottom). Wallboard screws have Phillips heads and are threaded all the way up the shaft. The drill has a clutch that disengages when the screw is properly seated. Because wallboard installers must move around a lot, many of them like to use the new cordless driver that runs on a rechargeable battery. If you buy an extra battery pack, you can charge one battery while you use the other.

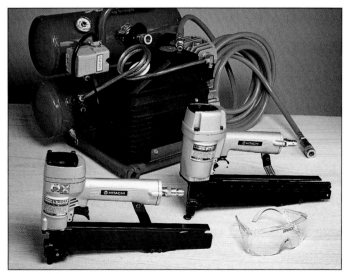

A pneumatic stapler (left) and a pneumatic nailer (right) are powered by an air compressor. Always wear safety goggles when using a power tool.

Gluing

Many woodworking joints can be fastened with glue alone. When a properly glued joint is stressed to the breaking point, it is often the wood surrounding the joint that fails, leaving the bonded surfaces intact. Although many types of glue are available, most finish carpentry jobs can be done with white polyvinyl resin glue or contact cement. Two exceptions are yellow aliphatic resin glue, which is used in high-heat situations, and the marine resin glues, such as resorcinol, which are used where waterproof joints are needed.

White Glue

Polyvinyl resin glue is a good all-around woodworking adhesive. It has replaced a variety of glues, some of which required mixing with water or heating in a pot. White glue is inexpensive, has a long shelf life, is transparent when dry, and has good gap-filling capability. The last is especially important to the strength of joints; although some gaps occur at visible edges, others occur in the heart of the joint, where they would not be detected until too late. White glue also sets up fast and dries quickly, which may or may not be an advantage depending on the project. A quick setup time is not desirable when many pieces must be assembled before clamping.

Clamping white-glue joints is a must. Mount the clamps as soon as possible, and don't flex the joint while it is drying. To prevent edge-glued pieces from buckling, mount bar clamps on opposite sides of the work. When the work is impossible to clamp, hold the joint in place with screws.

Yellow Glue

Aliphatic resin glue, or yellow glue, is often used in place of white glue, even when heat resistance is not a factor. The bonding is strong, and cleanup and sanding are easier than with white glue.

Contact Cement

This liquid adhesive is especially good for bonding large, flat materials, such as plastic laminate, to counters and table-tops. It can also be used to cement wood veneers in place. For very large jobs apply it with an inexpensive paint roller. For smaller projects simply brush it or pour it on and spread it with a serrated metal spreader.

Coat both surfaces to be joined and let the cement dry for 15 to 30 minutes before joining them. (Follow the manufacturer's instructions.) Then bring the pieces into contact. Once they touch they are bonded and cannot be repositioned. To break the bond see Working With Veneer, page 32.

To allow for accurate positioning, place a piece of paper between the two glued surfaces after they have set up. The paper lets you move the work around. When you are satisfied with the placement, slip the paper out. Alternatively, use lengths of dowels to roll the work into position.

To ensure contact apply pressure to each part of the glued surface—a heavy-duty rubber roller is made for this purpose—or pound the back of a wood block as you move it systematically over the work.

Mastic

This latex- or rubber-based cement, often called construction adhesive or paneling adhesive, has a heavier consistency than white glue or contact cement. It is applied directly from a tube with a caulking gun, or from a can with a serrated metal spreader. The sticky consistency of this glue enables it to adhere to vertical surfaces without running off; the glue will also conform to irregular surfaces. Use mastic to attach ceiling tiles, wall paneling, or floor tiles to furring strips or concrete.

Doweling

You can purchase dowels in various diameters and cut them to length. Put a 45-degree chamfer on each end of a dowel by drawing it across a sheet of medium sandpaper, twisting it as you do so. Then create a channel in the dowel to allow air and excess glue to escape when it is seated. Manufactured dowels have a spiral groove carved around the outside, but you can get comparable results by passing a regular dowel through a doweling jig made from a block of wood. Drill a hole in the block one size larger than the dowel; then drive an 8-penny (8d) nail into the block so that the point protrudes $1/32$ inch into the hole. Force each dowel through the hole several times to score it.

The hardest part of creating a good doweled joint is locating the sets of holes so that the dowels match up and the two pieces are properly aligned. There are three ways to do this: with dowel centers, a marking gauge, or a doweling jig.

For dowel centers, drill a hole in one workpiece only and put a dowel center of the same size into this hole. Carefully place the second workpiece in position over the hole containing the dowel center and press firmly. The point on the dowel center will mark the exact position for the hole in the second workpiece.

A marking gauge has many uses; marking dowel holes is one of them. Place the two workpieces side by side, with the surfaces to be joined face up. Set the marking gauge to the proper position and score a horizontal line across both pieces with one stroke. If you are using a marking gauge with two pins, you can scribe lines for two rows of dowels. Otherwise reset the gauge and scribe to mark as many rows as you need. For the vertical lines that create the cross-points for drilling, reset the gauge and scribe each workpiece individually.

A doweling jig is a viselike apparatus with interchangeable drill guides of various sizes. Once adjusted, the jig is clamped to each piece of work and a precise pattern of holes is drilled.

Simple variations on this machine are available, but most of them allow for drilling only one hole at a time. The Portalign® drill guide, a versatile tool that can be used as a doweling jig, attaches to most ¼-inch and ⅜-inch portable drill motors; it can be left in place when it isn't being used.

FINISHING THE EXTERIOR

Not only is exterior trim an aesthetic consideration, it allows the outside of a house to function as a weatherproof skin, so that a controlled temperature can be maintained inside. To protect your home from the elements, give top priority to completing the enclosure. Exterior finish carpentry is the means by which you seal out wind, snow, and rain, by covering the gaps where materials meet. Easy-to-follow instructions and illustrations give techniques for installing exterior window and door trim, finishing corners, and adding soffits and cornices. You will also learn how to build exterior stairs and railings.

Well-designed and carefully executed trim details, such as cornices and window and door trim, are what make this lovely Michigan home so striking.

AN OVERVIEW

Exterior finish work entails weatherproofing. Window and door trim must be correctly lapped to prevent leaks. Joints must fit tightly. And no matter how carefully you've lapped and fitted, caulking is essential to keep out wind and rain.

Minimizing Warpage

On a hot summer day, it is sometimes difficult to imagine what effects rain or snow will have on the exterior of a house, or how a blustery storm can drive moisture in through the seams and joints. Just remember when weatherproofing the exterior: It's nearly impossible to overdo it. Properly fastening the finish materials and then applying a moisture-resistant covering, such as paint, stain, or sealer, over every surface that is exposed to the elements is the best way to minimize deterioration and warpage.

Safety on the Job

Follow all the safety tips mentioned in the first chapter. In addition, there are a few precautions that are specific to this stage of the job. For example, you will need scaffolding and ladders for hillside or second-story construction. Set them up properly and use them correctly. Don't underestimate the potential hazard here. Make the effort to work safely; it saves time in the long run. The projects in this chapter are well within the abilities of the average do-it-yourselfer. For the sake of safety as well as efficiency, however, enlist the aid of friends or work alongside a professional if you feel uneasy about doing a job alone.

Materials

Exterior finish work is more exacting than rough framing, and the materials are more expensive. Give careful consideration to each piece of material that you select, cut, and install. Check through the materials after they have been delivered; of course you want to be economical, but it is always wise to have extra on hand. Mistakes in calculation and cutting are bound to occur, and the job will be delayed if you have to wait for additional supplies.

Trim Techniques

Techniques for installing exterior trim vary with the trim itself, the roof overhang, and the sequence of construction. The techniques for installing door and window casings vary with the wallcovering used. These techniques and the sequence of installation are explained in this chapter.

Measuring for Exterior Trim

The placement of exterior window and door trim, also known as casing, is best determined with a steel tape measure. Trim for doors is measured in the same way as trim for windows with sills that protrude from the building and extend beyond the bottom of the side casings. Measure the side casings first. Touch the tip of the tape measure to the windowsill and extend the tape vertically along the side jamb to just past the point where it intersects with the head jamb. Mark the cut line ¼ inch past the intersection. This allows for a ¼-inch reveal, or setback, from the edge of the jamb when the casing is installed. Once the side casings are cut and tacked in place, determine the length of the head casing by measuring the distance between the outside edges of the side casings. The usual practice is to add ½ inch to this dimension, to allow the head casing to extend ¼ inch beyond each side casing. See illustration on page 47.

The casings should be beveled on the bottom. If they are being installed over wood siding, they should be square on the top. If the trim is being installed with stucco or shingle siding, the side and head casings are usually mitered where they intersect. In this case, the measurement for the head casing is taken between the inside edges of the side casings, and the miter is cut from that dimension.

Other types of window frames require different procedures. Should a bottom casing be necessary on a window without a sill, its length is determined by measuring between the inside edges of the side jambs of the window and then adding ½ inch for reveal, plus twice the width of the side casing, plus ½ inch for overhang. Tack this piece in position, allowing ¼ inch of bottom-jamb reveal. Then determine the lengths of the side casings by measuring from the top edge of the bottom casing to ¼ inch past the bottom edge of the head jamb. Once these side casings are tacked in position, the head casing can be measured, cut, and installed as described for trimming windows with sills.

When exterior corner trim is necessary, take measurements with a steel tape. For inside corners, either 1 by 1 or 2 by 2 trim pieces are cut to a dimension that extends from the bottom of the starter piece of siding (or shingle course), or the top of the water table, to the bottom edge of the frieze block or rafter (or roof sheathing), or to the soffit. For outside corners the measurements are taken similarly, the exception being that the trim pieces are usually 1 by 4s overlapped at the vertical edges.

Measuring for cornice work is best done with a steel tape, although for precise dimensions—such as those between rafters—a folding rule with an extension slide may be preferable. Framing lumber is seldom straight and true, so take dimensions at both the top and the bottom of a rafter space when measuring for frieze boards or frieze blocks. When measuring for soffits take dimensions in several locations and cut to the narrowest one. This will reduce any necessary recutting. Gaps between the soffit and the siding will be covered by molding.

Measuring for Window and Door Trim

Horizontal Board Siding Wall Finish

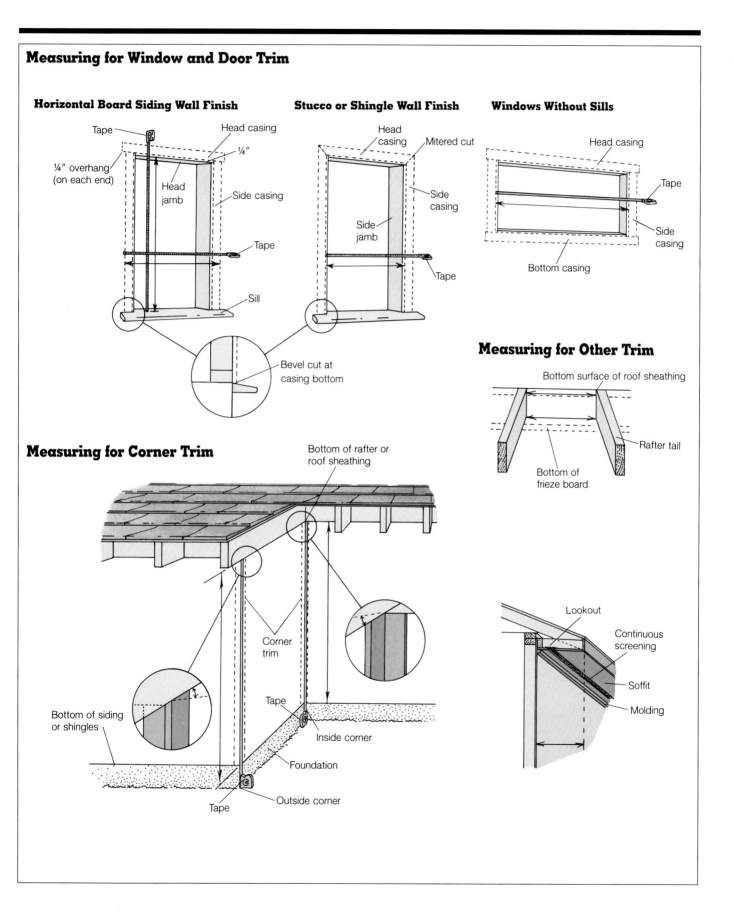

Tape

Head casing

¼"

¼" overhang (on each end)

Head jamb

Side casing

Tape

Sill

Bevel cut at casing bottom

Stucco or Shingle Wall Finish

Head casing

Mitered cut

Side jamb

Side casing

Tape

Windows Without Sills

Head casing

Tape

Side casing

Bottom casing

Measuring for Other Trim

Bottom surface of roof sheathing

Rafter tail

Bottom of frieze board

Measuring for Corner Trim

Bottom of rafter or roof sheathing

Corner trim

Tape

Inside corner

Foundation

Bottom of siding or shingles

Tape

Outside corner

Lookout

Continuous screening

Soffit

Molding

EXTERIOR WINDOW TRIM

Whether or not you need exterior window casing depends on the window frame and on the wallcovering. Nearly all wood-framed windows require exterior casing. Metal-framed windows often do not, particularly when they are used with stucco, brick, or stone wallcovering.

When to Install It

The casing for wood-framed windows is installed before or after the wallcovering, depending on what type of wallcovering is used. With shingle, stucco, brick, and stone, the casing is usually installed first. With horizontal or vertical board siding, the casing can be installed first or last. With plywood siding the casing is usually installed last. See illustrations on pages 49 to 51.

Metal windows with nailing flanges should be installed before the wallcovering. A casing may or may not be required. With shingle the casing is optional; if you elect to use it, it should be installed before the wallcovering. With horizontal and vertical board siding and plywood, the casing is installed last. With stucco, brick, and stone, no casing is used.

If your house is of a unique design that calls for unusual windows, wallcoverings, or casing procedures, ask a knowledgeable source to help you to determine whether, and when, to install casing.

Installing Casings on Wood-Framed Windows

Now that you know what casing to install, when to install it, and how to measure it, you're ready to start. The following discussion deals with wood-framed windows. Casing for metal windows is discussed on page 49. As part of taking the measurements, you will have marked the reveal from the edges of all jambs for positioning the casing (see page 46).

In addition to the casing on a wood-framed window, a trim strip—called an apron—is often installed beneath the window-sill on houses with a wood wallcovering. The apron, usually made of 1 by 3 or 1 by 4 stock, is used to close the gap between the underside of the windowsill and the adjoining wallcovering. Cut the apron the same length as the sill, and caulk the gap before installing the apron.

Square Cuts

Square-cut casings are recommended with board siding. Using a sliding bevel, determine the angle of cut where the bottom of the casing meets the sloped windowsill. Make this cut at one end of a piece of stock meant for that particular window. Then measure from the short end of the bevel and cut this piece to length. Tack it in place and repeat the procedure for the other side piece. To complete the job cut the top piece to length, position it, and tack it in place. Make any necessary adjustments and nail the pieces down.

Mitered Cuts

A variation of this procedure uses mitered cuts at the upper corners. Use this technique with stucco and shingle wallcoverings.

Start by cutting the side casings. At one end of the piece of stock, make the bevel bottom cut. Then mark the measured dimension from the short edge of the bevel to the inside of the miter. Cut the miter—be sure to cut in the proper direction—and tack the piece in place.

Cut the other side casing in the same way, but do not tack this piece in place yet. Now cut the mating miter (the head casing) for the first side casing on the remaining piece of stock and test it against the side casing miter to determine the fit. If this is satisfactory, hold the head casing in place and mark the length of the side casing at the short point of the miter on the opposite end of the head casing stock. Cut the miter, tack the second side casing in place, then position the head casing. As with all casings, make any minor adjustments to the mitered cuts and the position of the pieces before you complete the nailing.

Caulking

If the casings are to be painted, small gaps or cracks can be caulked first. Casings that are to be stained or sealed with a clear material must fit together well, because most caulks will show through and be unsightly. (A limited range of colored caulks is available. One of these may match the stained or sealed wood.)

Nailing

Hot-dipped galvanized common and box nails are most often used for exterior applications. Both are weather resistant and hold well. Finishing nails are not usually used on exteriors; their holding capability is inferior to that of common and box nails.

There is some controversy about galvanized nails. The galvanizing can be damaged by repeated hammering, and rust can form on the nail head and run down the casing. On painted exteriors the nail heads are covered, but on unpainted surfaces the rust can stain the wallcovering. In such situations aluminum, electroplated, or stainless steel (very expensive) nails are sometimes used. It's also possible to set the nails slightly and then caulk the cavity to seal it; of course, this is effective only if matching caulk or wood filler can be obtained.

As a rule, nails should be evenly spaced between 12 inches and 18 inches apart. The top and bottom nails should be about 1 inch from the ends of the casing. Closer nailing may be necessary where the stock is bowed or otherwise irregular.

Installing Square-Cut Window Trim

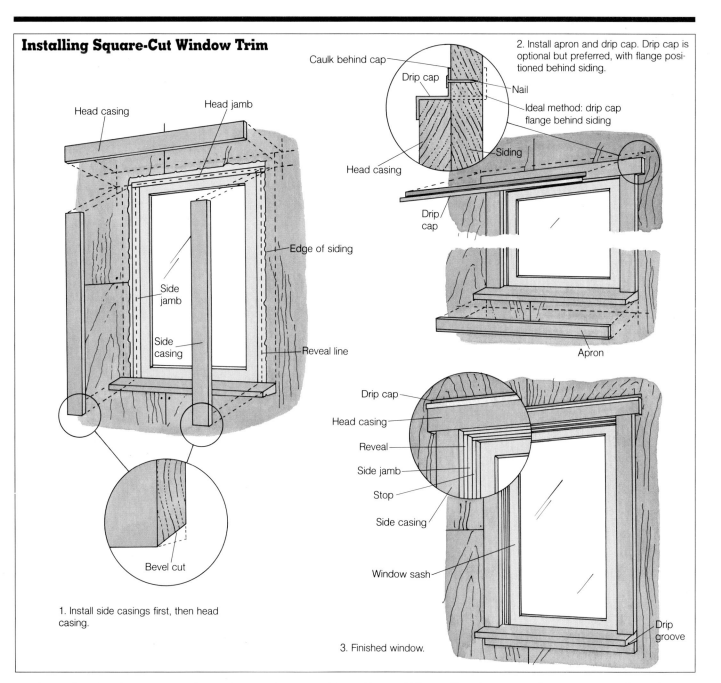

Head casing

Head jamb

Side jamb

Side casing

Edge of siding

Reveal line

Bevel cut

1. Install side casings first, then head casing.

2. Install apron and drip cap. Drip cap is optional but preferred, with flange positioned behind siding.

Caulk behind cap

Drip cap

Nail

Ideal method: drip cap flange behind siding

Head casing

Siding

Drip cap

Apron

Drip cap

Head casing

Reveal

Side jamb

Stop

Side casing

Window sash

Drip groove

3. Finished window.

The preferred nailing pattern is to have the outside and inside nails opposite each other. When driving a nail close to the edge or end of the casing, predrill a hole to avoid splitting the wood.

As an added refinement on mitered corners, nails can be driven through the edges of the side casings—near the top—into each end of the head casing, and also through the top edges of the head casing down into the end of each side casing. This will tighten the mitered joints and help to keep them from separating. Use finishing nails on these corners, set and sealed for appearance.

Installing Casings on Metal-Framed Windows

Casings are not required on metal-framed windows when the wallcovering is stucco, brick, or stone, since the metal frame acts as the finish for these materials. However, wood casing is occasionally used to frame a metal window when the wallcovering is shingle. In this instance, the casing is chosen primarily to enhance the design; it is not necessary for weatherproofing.

Installing Mitered-Cut Window Trim

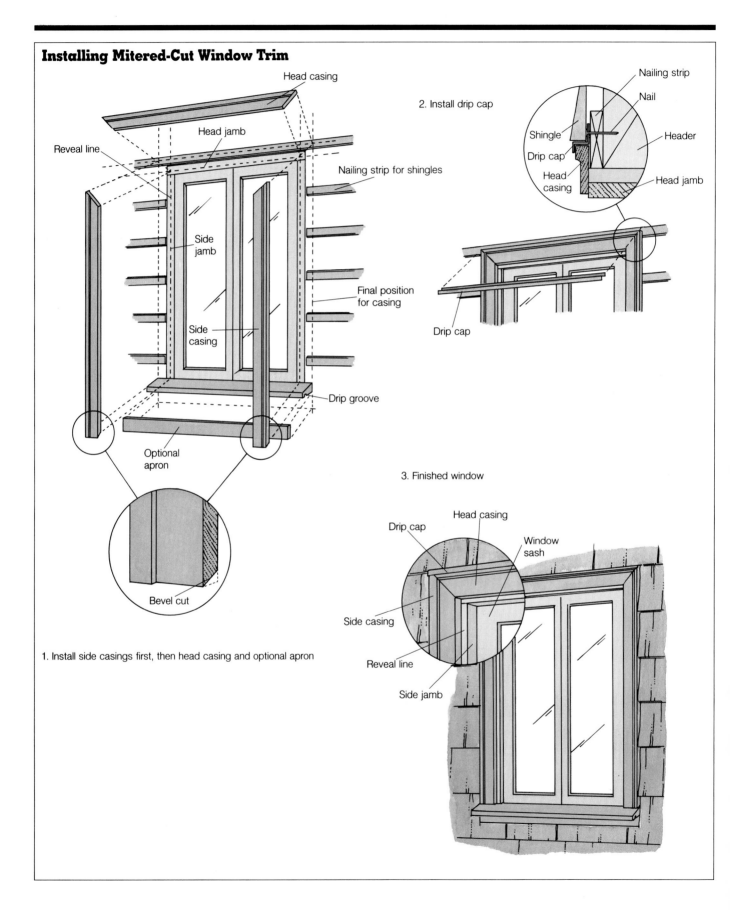

Head casing

Reveal line

Head jamb

Nailing strip for shingles

Side jamb

Final position for casing

Side casing

Drip groove

Optional apron

Bevel cut

1. Install side casings first, then head casing and optional apron

2. Install drip cap

Nailing strip

Nail

Shingle

Drip cap

Header

Head casing

Head jamb

Drip cap

3. Finished window

Drip cap

Head casing

Window sash

Side casing

Reveal line

Side jamb

Installing Trim on Metal-Framed Sliding Windows

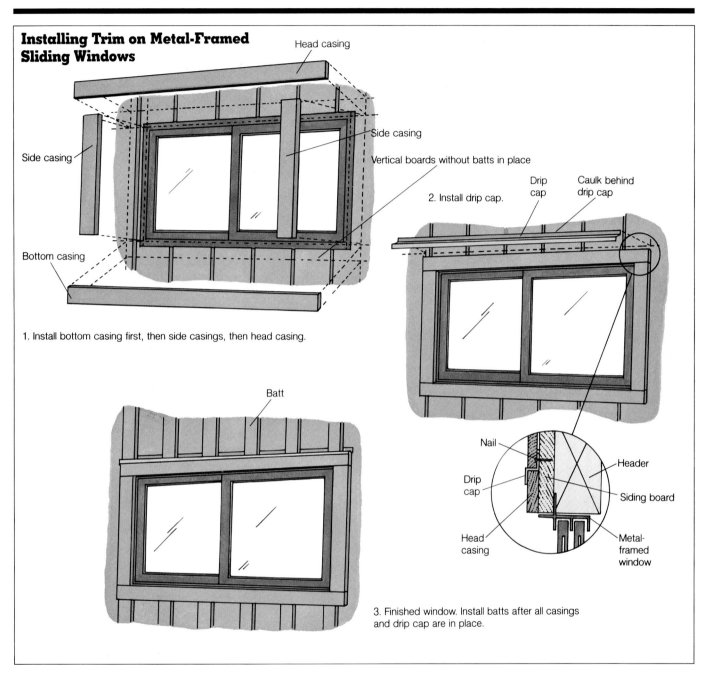

Head casing

Side casing

Side casing

Bottom casing

1. Install bottom casing first, then side casings, then head casing.

Vertical boards without batts in place

2. Install drip cap.

Drip cap

Caulk behind drip cap

Batt

Nail

Drip cap

Head casing

Header

Siding board

Metal-framed window

3. Finished window. Install batts after all casings and drip cap are in place.

Wood casing can also be used with stucco; again, this is an option and not a necessity. Before the stucco is applied, the casing is nailed over a previously installed board, called a ground, which is narrower than the casing. This allows stucco to squeeze behind the casing and seal the joint.

When board or plywood siding is used, the casing is usually installed after the siding is in place. All sides of the window, including the bottom, are cased out. The installation procedure is the same as that for wood-framed windows, except that there is a bottom piece of casing to fit, and there is no reveal on the wood jamb to hold to, only the metal window frame. The bottom casing is installed first. It acts much like the sill in a wood-framed window. However, because the bottom casing is not slanted like a sill, the side casings do not take a bevel cut.

EXTERIOR DOOR TRIM

The procedures and techniques used to choose and install window casings are essentially the same ones that are used for doors. The type of casing is determined largely by the wall-covering, and the style of finish is dictated by the desired appearance.

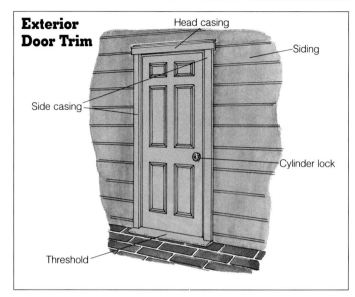

Exterior Door Trim

Head casing
Siding
Side casing
Cylinder lock
Threshold

Types of Doors

Several types of exterior doors are used in residential construction. The most common is the wood-framed swinging door (see illustration at right). The bottom member of this type of door is called the threshold, which is analogous to a windowsill. This type of door is usually cased out in the same way as a wood-framed window. The difference is the length of the side casings.

The sliding glass door is usually metal framed, but some models come with a wood frame. This type of door is usually cased out in the same way as a metal-framed window. A bottom casing is used with certain wallcoverings, such as board siding, and no casing is used with others, such as stucco, brick, and stone.

The trim procedure required for garage doors is nearly the same as that for swinging doors. The difference is that there is no threshold on which to set the side casings, so they are straight cut to finish even with the bottom of the side jambs. See illustration at left.

Most pet doors come with all the materials required to complete and weatherproof the installation. Should you choose to construct your own pet door, trim the exterior side as for a regular swinging door, in either threshold or picture frame style. Take care to weatherproof the door adequately without hampering its free movement.

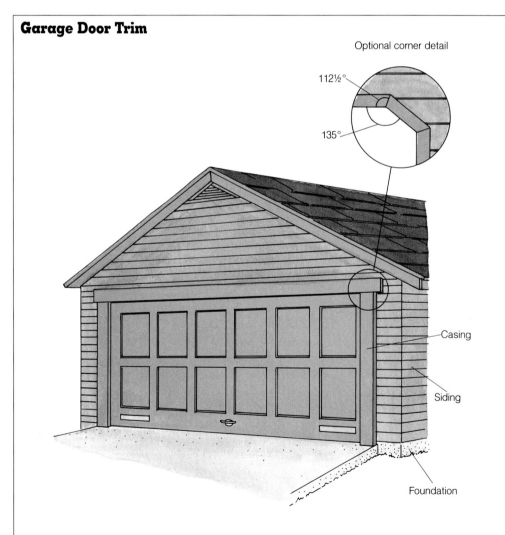

Garage Door Trim

Optional corner detail

112½°
135°

Casing
Siding
Foundation

Corners, cornices, and gutters and downspouts are elements of exterior finish work that are functional and lend polish to the outside of your home. The illustration at right is an overview of these and other exterior trim elements.

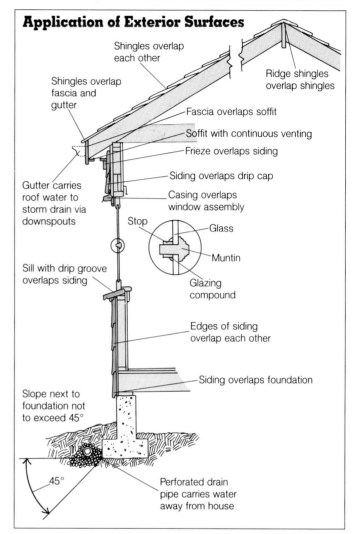

Application of Exterior Surfaces

Shingles overlap each other

Shingles overlap fascia and gutter

Ridge shingles overlap shingles

Fascia overlaps soffit

Soffit with continuous venting

Frieze overlaps siding

Gutter carries roof water to storm drain via downspouts

Siding overlaps drip cap

Casing overlaps window assembly

Stop

Glass

Muntin

Sill with drip groove overlaps siding

Glazing compound

Edges of siding overlap each other

Siding overlaps foundation

Slope next to foundation not to exceed 45°

45°

Perforated drain pipe carries water away from house

Corners

All buildings have outside corners; many buildings have inside corners as well. (An outside corner angles out; an inside corner angles in.) Corners are trimmed to create a finished appearance and to provide additional weather protection. Different types of trim are used for each type of corner. Most treatments are also dictated by the wallcovering used, although several different treatments are possible for each wallcovering. See illustration on page 54.

Outside Corners

The finish on an outside corner is largely determined by the wallcovering. With horizontal board siding the options are to miter each course where it meets at the corner or to make butt cuts on the siding and cover the corner with trim. For beveled siding it is also possible to apply metal corners to each course of siding.

Shingles are usually overlapped at the corners, alternating the lap with each course.

A less common option is to trim the corners with vertical boards. Vertical board siding is treated like shingle.

Trim pieces used at outside corners are installed after the wallcovering is in place. The trim extends from the bottom edge of the siding to the bottom edge of the frieze board or block. First, measure and cut a 1 by 4 (or whatever size of board is appropriate). Tack it in place at the corner, making sure that one edge is even with the plane of the intersecting wall. Next, cut the mating piece and hold it in position against the first piece, covering the edge. If the two boards fit together well, finish nailing the first piece. Then nail the second piece in its final position. If the fit is not acceptable, make the necessary adjustments.

If there are no frieze boards or blocks, the trim pieces should extend to the roof sheathing. This installation is simple, provided that you recognized the need for slightly longer stock when you ordered the material. Taking the time to visualize the completed details in advance is an important part of efficient ordering.

For a slightly different appearance, install a quarter-round trim piece at the intersection of the two 1-by boards. This gives a rounded look to the corner.

Inside Corners

The sequence for installing trim on an inside corner depends on the wallcovering. When horizontal board siding or shingle is used, it is common to install a square trim piece before the siding is applied. This gives a more finished appearance. Trim for vertical board siding and plywood is usually installed after the wallcovering is in place.

At an inside corner 1 by 1s are used to cover the joint between two pieces of vertical siding or plywood. With horizontal siding and shingle, 2 by 2s are standard. They are nailed in place before the wallcovering is installed. This produces a reveal that is pleasing in appearance. Occasionally a 1 by 1 will be installed after horizontal siding is in place. This is acceptable but less attractive.

Nailing

The nails used for corner trim should be of the same type, and spaced in the same way, as those used for window and door casing. However, they should be smaller. When fastening a 1 by 1, nail it in both directions to attach it securely to the corner.

Corner Trim Styles

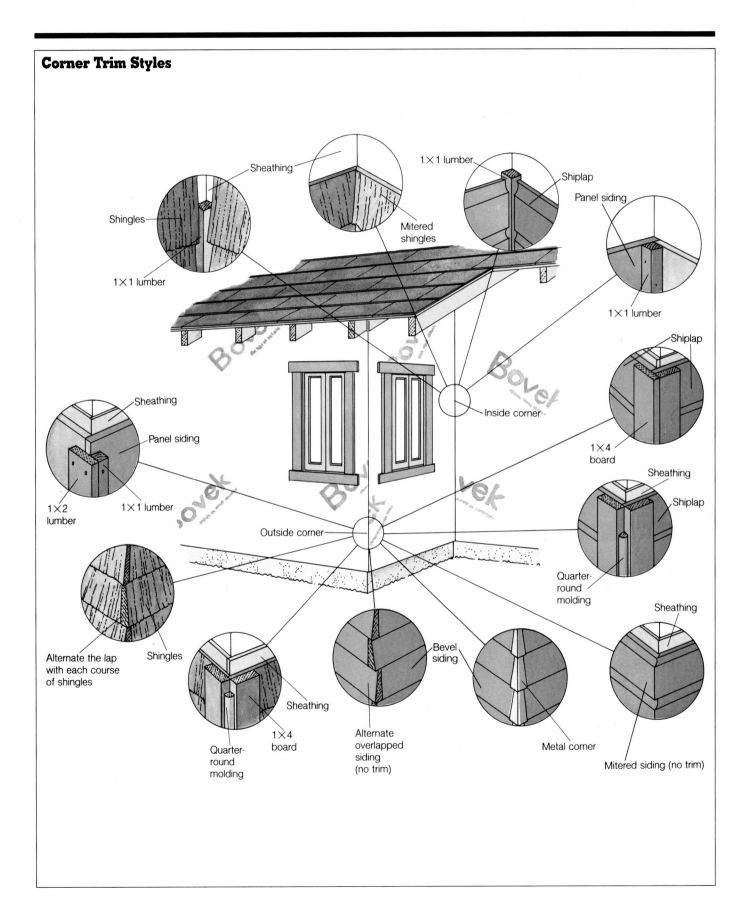

Sheathing

Shingles

1×1 lumber

Mitered shingles

1×1 lumber

Shiplap

Panel siding

1×1 lumber

Shiplap

1×4 board

Sheathing

Shiplap

Quarter-round molding

Inside corner

Sheathing

Panel siding

1×2 lumber

1×1 lumber

Outside corner

Alternate the lap with each course of shingles

Shingles

Quarter-round molding

1×4 board

Sheathing

Alternate overlapped siding (no trim)

Bevel siding

Metal corner

Sheathing

Mitered siding (no trim)

Cornices

A cornice is the trim that covers the joint where the roof and walls meet. The way in which the roof was framed determines the cornice treatment. If the intersection of the roof and walls forms a right angle, a horizontal cornice is used. At gable ends, where the intersection forms an acute angle, a raked cornice is used.

The overhang of the rafters determines the width of the eaves. If the rafters are not long enough to give the desired overhang, you can extend them by attaching tail rafters on the horizontal eaves or lookout rafters at the gable ends. However, this must be done before the roofing is laid.

All cornices, regardless of type, are classified as either open or closed. In an open cornice the spaces between the rafter ends (or the tail rafters) are left open. In a closed cornice, also called a boxed cornice, a panel known as a soffit covers the underside of the rafters. The soffit is attached directly to the rafters or mounted on the lookouts.

With any type of cornice work, the rafter spaces must be ventilated to prevent condensation from forming on the underside of the roof sheathing. The moisture would deteriorate the wood members and the insulation in the attic or rafter spaces. Proper ventilation is achieved in various ways, depending on the particular cornice used.

Open Cornices

The open cornice is relatively easy and inexpensive to build. Its main features are the frieze and the fascia. See illustration.

The Frieze

This is a 2-by board that closes the gap between the last course of siding and the rafters. Cut a rabbet on the bottom edge of the frieze to fit over the top of the last course of siding and notch the upper edge of the frieze to fit snugly around the rafters. To cover the remaining space between the frieze and the underside of the roof, cut frieze blocks from 1-by stock. Nail the blocks to the frieze and to cleats that match the thickness of the frieze. If the gap is not too large, you can use sections of crown molding instead of frieze blocks. If the siding already reaches to the bottom of the rafters, all you need is frieze blocks. Back-prime all pieces before nailing them in place.

The Fascia

To trim the ends of the rafters, rip a 1-by board so that it covers the edge of the roof and extends ½ inch below the rafters. Any joints in this board must occur over rafter ends so that each section can be nailed securely. To prevent splitting, drill pilot holes for the nails. When you turn a corner, miter the ends of the fascia so that the joints are tight. Be sure to back-prime the fascia before attaching it.

On raked cornices nail the fascia so that it is snug against the underside of the roofing. The fascia should cover and extend at least 1 inch below the nailing board. (It should extend 2 inches if the roof pitch is steeper than 6 in 12.)

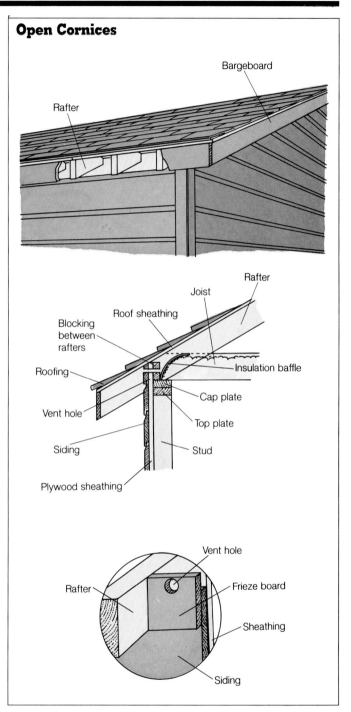

Open Cornices

Bargeboard

Rafter

Rafter

Joist

Roof sheathing

Blocking between rafters

Roofing

Insulation baffle

Vent hole

Cap plate

Siding

Top plate

Plywood sheathing

Stud

Vent hole

Rafter

Frieze board

Sheathing

Siding

Closed Cornices

In a closed, or boxed, cornice, the area between and underneath the rafters is closed off by a panel called a soffit. Except for the soffit and its supports, the closed cornice is the same as the open cornice.

Closed Cornices

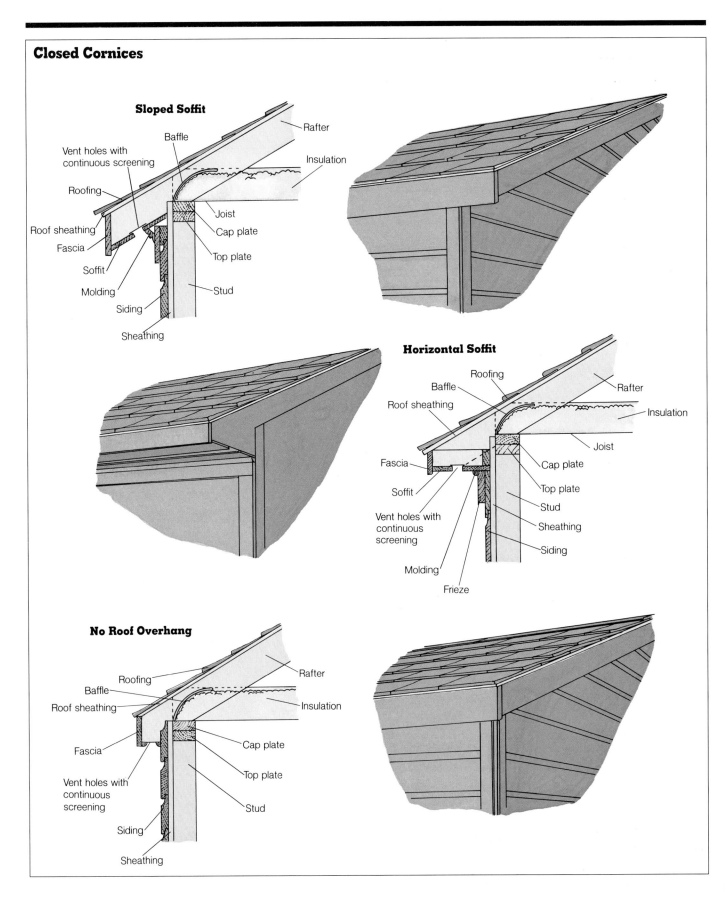

Sloped Soffit

Rafter

Baffle

Vent holes with continuous screening

Insulation

Roofing

Roof sheathing

Joist

Fascia

Cap plate

Soffit

Top plate

Molding

Stud

Siding

Sheathing

Horizontal Soffit

Roofing

Baffle

Rafter

Roof sheathing

Insulation

Fascia

Joist

Soffit

Cap plate

Top plate

Vent holes with continuous screening

Stud

Sheathing

Molding

Siding

Frieze

No Roof Overhang

Roofing

Rafter

Baffle

Roof sheathing

Insulation

Fascia

Cap plate

Top plate

Vent holes with continuous screening

Stud

Siding

Sheathing

The Lookouts

The first step in building a closed cornice is to attach a lookout to each eave rafter; these lookouts support the soffit and strengthen the overhang. Use 2 by 4 stock. Toenail the lookouts into the wall sheathing and facenail them to the rafters.

The Soffit

This can be made of ⅜-inch plywood if the rafters are no more than 16 inches apart. Use ½-inch plywood if the rafters are more than 16 inches apart. Measure the width of the soffit, subtracting 2 inches to allow for ventilation (described below). Measure and cut the plywood to length, then cut each piece lengthwise into two.

Tack the front piece of plywood against the fascia. Install a continuous strip of 2½-inch-wide screening along the rear edge of the plywood and staple it at each rafter. Position the other piece of plywood 2 inches behind the first piece and next to the sheathing. Nail both pieces of plywood completely.

The Frieze

In a closed cornice as in an open one, a frieze covers the space above the top course of siding. Cut the frieze boards out of 2-by stock. Cut a rabbet along the bottom edge of each board to lap over the top edge of the siding. Butt the top of the frieze against the soffit.

If there is no nailing board on the gable, nail blocks to the siding between the lookout rafters. The angle and position of the blocks must allow for a raked soffit—the bottom edge of the blocks must be level with the bottom edge of the

lookout rafters. Cut and nail the gable soffit in place as you did the eave soffit, but stop at the point where it meets the return cornice.

The Fascia

Cap the ends of the rafters by nailing a fascia board all around the cornice. Miter the corners and make sure that all the joints are positioned over rafter ends.

In a cornice where there is no roof overhang, fasten the fascia to the rafter ends so that it overlaps the upper edge of the top siding board. This eliminates the need for a soffit. In this hybrid between an open and a closed cornice, the closure is screening instead of a soffit. Since the attic (or rafter space) must be ventilated, the rafters must overhang the siding by an amount sufficient to allow the air to flow. A 2-inch opening is standard with this type of cornice. Cover it with continuous screening or mesh to keep out insects and birds.

Gutters and Downspouts

Usually made from galvanized metal, plastic, or aluminum, gutters are designed to catch rainwater running off the roof, and downspouts direct the flow of water away from the foundation. There is no firm rule governing the location of downspouts, but they are normally placed at the end of a gutter and not where they will be an eyesore—right next to a window, for example.

Gutters and downspouts come in a variety of sizes. Use the following guide to determine what size to use. As a rule

of thumb, you should install one downspout for every 600 square feet of roof or for every 20 to 30 feet of gutter.

Square feet: 750 to 1,000
Gutter: 4 inch
Downspout diameter: 3 inch

Square feet: 1,400 to 2,500
Gutter: 5 inch
Downspout diameter: 4 inch

Installing Gutters

Gutters usually come in 10-foot lengths. Each section is fitted into the next with a slip joint that snaps into place. All the joints should be caulked to prevent leaks.

Gutters are hung on the fascia board covering the exposed rafter ends, or on the rafter ends themselves if there is no fascia. They are attached with straps nailed under the roofing material at the eaves, with spikes that fit through a ferrule in the gutter, or with brackets nailed to the fascia. Start installing the gutters at the end farthest from the downspout. This starting end should be the high point of the run, and the end of the gutter should fit snugly under the overhang of the roofing material.

For proper drainage the gutter should slope ½ inch for every 10 feet of run. If the run is more than 20 feet, position the high point in the center and install a downspout at each end.

To mark the slope drive a small nail at the high point, allow a ½-inch slope for every 10 feet of run, and drive another nail at the low point. Snap a chalk line between the two points and place the top of the gutter along this line.

For gutters made from heavy-gauge metal, such as galvanized steel, place hangers 4 feet apart; for lighter aluminum, 3 feet apart; for plastic, about 30 inches apart.

If the gutters will have to support snow, strengthen the connections with self-tapping metal screws. Remember to use screws that match the metal you are working with. Don't use galvanized screws with aluminum, or vice versa, because the dissimilar metals set up an electrolytic reaction that causes rapid corrosion.

Close up the ends of the gutters with slip-on caps and caulk all seams carefully.

Installing Downspouts

Sections of downspouts are joined to each other and to the gutter with slip connections that must be carefully caulked. A series of elbows is usually used to make the downspout conform to the wall of the house. This is sturdier and more attractive than having it run from the gutter straight to the ground.

The bottom of the downspout should be fitted with an elbow connection to direct the flow of water away from the house. To prevent erosion there should be a splash block at the base of the downspout.

To keep a downspout from becoming clogged with leaves and other debris, make an inexpensive trap by fitting a cylinder of window screening tightly into the hole at the top of the downspout. The cylinder should be slightly higher than the gutter is deep, to prevent leaves from washing over the top of the screen.

EXTERIOR STAIRS AND RAILINGS

The style of the stairs has a considerable impact on the overall appearance of a house. Several basic styles of stairway are common to residential construction. Each has its own look, appropriate uses, and method of fabrication. Your choice will be based on considerations of design as well as of practicality.

Exterior Stairs

With each style of stairs comes the choice of how to cut and assemble the parts. One method is to notch the stringers in a sawtooth pattern so that treads can be fastened to them to serve as steps. If risers are used, they can be fastened to the stringers too. The stringers are included in the width of the stairway and do not protrude beyond the length of the tread. Stairways constructed in this manner typically require more support than other types of stairways.

Another method is to mortise the stringers so that the treads and risers fit into them. These stairs require less support than those with notched stringers.

Still another method is to use cleats or metal angles to support the treads on each stringer. Here again less support is needed.

Is one method better than the others? No; it is mostly a matter of personal choice. The notched-stringer method is usually faster; once the layout is completed, the cutting process moves along rapidly. Mortising stringers or attaching cleats or metal angles to them both take more time.

The low end of exterior stair stringers ordinarily sits on a raised sill, which is elevated above ground level by a concrete pad. At the top of the stairs, the stringers are attached to deck or landing support members or to posts. Conditions vary, so exact fastening details must be determined at the job site.

Determining the rise and run—the relationship between the height of the riser and the width of the tread—is done in the same way for all three methods. In the explanation that follows, the notched-stringer method is used as an example. See illustration on page 59.

Notched Stringers

The staircase in this example leads from a garden to a second-story deck; it is parallel with and close to the side of the house. The lowest step will be the concrete pad mentioned above. The height of this pad will be the same as the height of each of the risers.

Determining the Number of Steps

In constructing stairs the first task is to determine the rise and run. There is a given relationship between the height of the riser and the width of the tread (front to back). The sum of these two figures should be between 17 and 18 inches for stairs that are the most comfortable and safe to use. Thus, if the riser height is 7 inches, the tread width will be 10 inches; if the riser height is 6 inches, the tread width will be 11 inches. Risers should be between 6 and 7½ inches high and treads between 10 and 11 inches wide. When the risers are much higher than this and the treads are narrower, the stairs are uncomfortable to use and can be dangerous. The same is true if the risers are much lower and the treads are wider. Keep in mind that the lower the riser, the greater the number of risers and the greater the length of the stairway. If space is limited, the risers must be made as high as these rules permit.

To determine the rise and run, first find the difference in elevation between the two levels. In calculating the total rise of a stairway, always measure from the top of the finished surface of the lower (or ground) floor to the top of the finished surface of the upper floor. (If the decking has not yet been laid, add the thickness of the decking material). One way to do this is with a story pole, which is simply a straight piece of 1 by 2 or 1 by 4. Set one end of the pole on the ground where the bottom of the stairs will be. Hold the pole vertical and mark on it the location of the top of the stairs, in this case the second-story deck.

The distance between the ground and the finished deck level is the total rise. Say that this distance is 108 inches, and that the risers are to be about 7 inches high. To determine the number of risers, including the concrete step, divide the total rise by the approximate height of the risers and drop any fraction. To find the exact height of each riser, divide the total rise by the number of risers. Dividing 108 inches by 7 gives 15.43. Dropping the fraction gives 15 risers. Dividing of 108 by 15 gives 7.2, or 7¼ inches as the height of each riser. To determine the tread width, for example, subtract 7¼ from the arbitrary figure 17½ (halfway between the recommended 17-to-18-inch sum of the rise and run), which gives 10¼ inches.

The total run is the total length of the stringers. To find this figure multiply the width of each tread by one less than the number of risers (because there is always one less tread). In this example, multiplying 10¼ inches by 14 (15 risers minus 1) gives 143½ inches as the total run.

Marking the Stringers

Select-grade, pressure-treated 2 by 12 lumber is the best material for stringers. Select-grade lumber has no knots, cracks, splits, curves, or other defects; 2 by 12s are used for strength and because it is easy to lay them out with the framing square. For a stairway about 3 feet wide, two stringers are adequate. For stairs more than 3 feet wide, add a central supporting stringer.

With your figures close at hand, mark the cuts for the first stringer. Position it on sawhorses; then set the framing square so that the tongue (the short leg) measures the height of the riser and the blade (the long leg) measures the width of the tread. See illustration on page 59. Scribe the outline of the square onto the stringer. Continue this process until you

Exterior Stairs

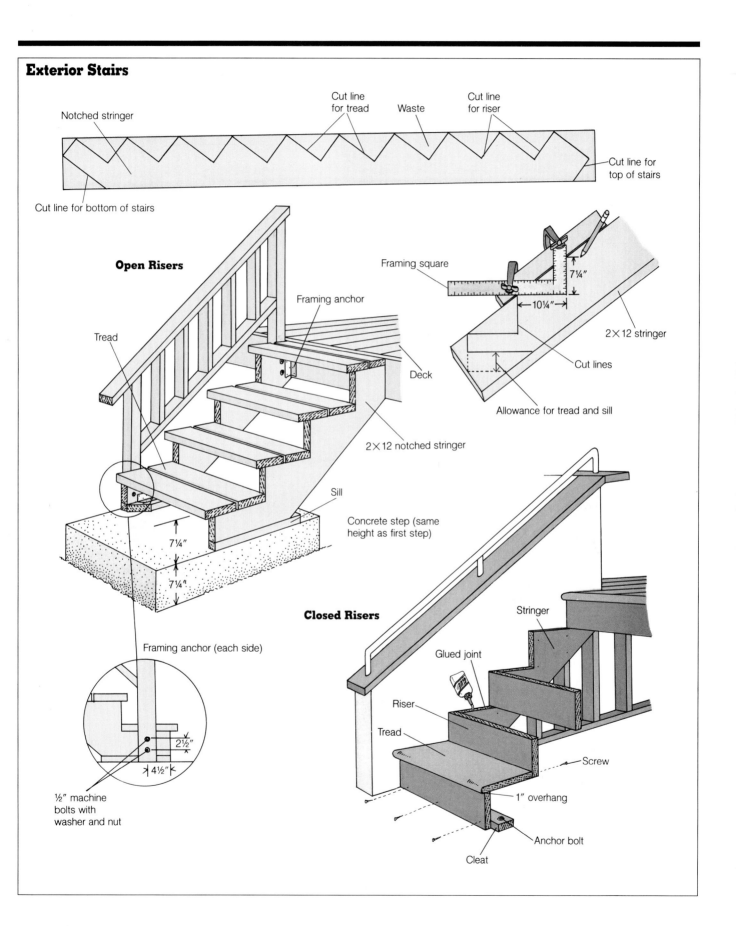

Notched stringer

Cut line for tread

Waste

Cut line for riser

Cut line for top of stairs

Cut line for bottom of stairs

Open Risers

Framing anchor

Tread

Framing square

7¼"

10¼"

2 × 12 stringer

Cut lines

Deck

Allowance for tread and sill

2 × 12 notched stringer

Sill

7¼"

Concrete step (same height as first step)

7¼"

Closed Risers

Framing anchor (each side)

Stringer

Glued joint

Riser

Tread

2½"

4½"

½" machine bolts with washer and nut

Screw

1" overhang

Anchor bolt

Cleat

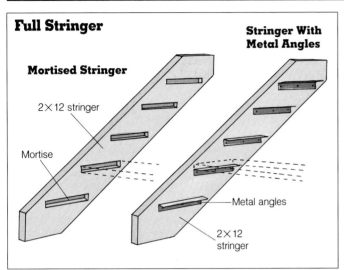

Full Stringer

Mortised Stringer

2 × 12 stringer

Mortise

Stringer With Metal Angles

Metal angles

2 × 12 stringer

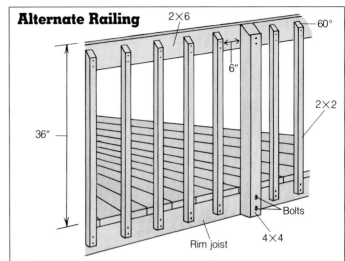

Alternate Railing

2 × 6

60°

6"

36"

2 × 2

Bolts

4 × 4

Rim joist

have marked the stringer with all the riser heights and tread widths. Then, to make the bottom step the same height as the others, trim the bottom of the stringer by the thickness of the tread material plus the thickness of the sill on which the stringers will sit.

Test the first stringer in position to see whether it fits properly before cutting the other stringer. Use a carpenter's level to make sure that the horizontal cuts are indeed horizontal, so that the treads will be level. Make any necessary adjustments. Then use the first stringer as a pattern to cut the other stringer. Lay the first stringer on the second piece of stock, clamp the two pieces together, and draw the cut lines.

After the stringers have been notched for treads and risers, you should determine whether any other cuts are required at the upper ends in order to attach them to existing framing members. If so, make the necessary cuts.

Installing the Stringers

Position the lower end of one stringer on the sill in the proper location. Move the stringer into position at the upper end. Toenail the lower end into the sill with several 8-penny (8d) hot-dipped galvanized nails, alternating sides. Then fasten the upper end with toenails, framing anchors, or joist hangers. For added strength attach framing anchors to the sill joint. Repeat the process with the other stringer, making sure that the distance between the stringers is consistent and appropriate for the length of the tread.

Cutting and Fastening the Treads and Risers

Select-grade, pressure-treated 2-by lumber is best for exterior treads. In open stairways when balusters are fastened directly to notched stringers instead of to a lower rail, the treads are usually flush with the outside edge of the outer stringers. Otherwise, the treads often extend beyond the edge of the stringers by approximately 1 inch, giving a better appearance. When selecting tread

stock allow for about 1 inch of overhang at the front, or nose, of the tread.

Where risers are appropriate, such as in enclosed stairways and formal entry stairways, use a medium-hard wood for both the treads and risers. The most common tread stock is $1\frac{3}{16}$ inches thick; risers are usually made from 1-by stock. When risers are used, they are installed before the treads. Starting at the bottom, install the first riser below the position of the first tread. Install the second riser next. Then butt the tread up against the second riser, using mastic adhesive and screws driven through the back of the riser into the tread, to give added support. Facenail the tread with 8d nails near the front edge of the riser beneath it. Follow the same sequence—riser, then tread in front of it—for the rest of the stairway.

Full Stringers

When cleats or angles are used to hold the treads, the stringers are laid out as described above. The cleats, made from 1-by lumber or metal angles, are in-

stalled to the drawn lines using $1\frac{1}{2}$-inch screws. Predrill the cleat holes. Cutting is necessary only at the bottom of the stringers, where they sit on the sills, and at the top, at the deck level in the example. The tread stock is cut to the net dimension desired, and then positioned and fastened. See illustration above, left.

For a mortised stringer, follow the same layout procedure as described above. Then draw cutting lines for the mortises by tracing around the end of a piece of tread stock. Cut the mortises $\frac{1}{2}$ inch deep. After assembling all the treads between the stringers with yellow aliphatic resin and $\frac{1}{4}$-inch by 3-inch lag screws, install the complete staircase in place.

Exterior Railings

A railing provides the finishing touch to a stairway or deck. It is also required by the building code and must meet code standards. There must be no gap between the balusters large enough for children to insert their heads—6 inches is the usual maximum distance allowed—and there must be a handrail at a comfortable and safe height—usually a minimum of 34 inches above the tread and 36 inches above the deck. Check the local code for the requirements in your area.

There are many styles of railings. One popular style consists of posts, a handrail, a lower rail, and balusters. To give a neat appearance and hold the posts and balusters firmly in place, it is a good idea to cut a ⅜-inch-deep groove in the underside of the handrail. Allow for this measurement on the plans. See illustration.

Posts

Because they are the backbone of the railing, posts must be sturdy. They must also be firmly anchored to either the stringers or the deck joists. Choose 4 by 4s in an appearance-grade stock suitable for outdoor use. If you're building a railing to enclose a second-story deck, as in the example, set one post (the newel) at the bottom of the stairs, one at the top of the stairs, posts equally spaced 3 to 6 feet apart on the stairs, one post at each corner of the deck, and posts at 6-foot intervals between the corners. Use tighter spacing if the posts are less than 4 by 4, if the railing will be pieced (see below), or if you want a sturdier-looking railing.

Cut the posts to a length that will support the handrail at the required height. Cut a ¾-inch notch at the base of each post and fit the post against the stringer before attaching the treads. Cut a tenon on the top of each post to match the groove in the underside of the handrail. Drill the posts, stringers, and joists to accept at least two ⅜-inch carriage bolts or lag screws and secure the posts in position.

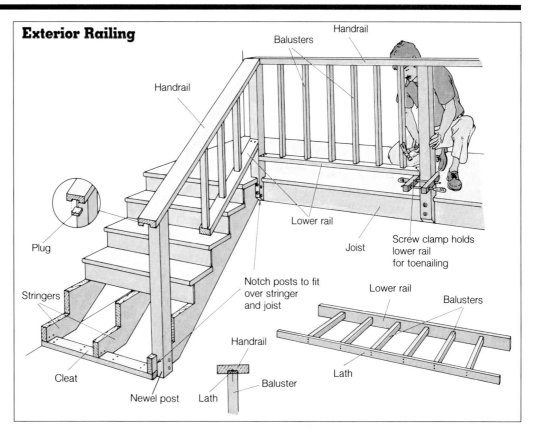

Exterior Railing

Handrail
Balusters
Handrail
Handrail
Plug
Lower rail
Joist
Screw clamp holds lower rail for toenailing
Stringers
Notch posts to fit over stringer and joist
Lower rail
Balusters
Cleat
Handrail
Lath
Newel post
Lath
Baluster

Rails

Use 2 by 6 stock for the handrail if you want it to overlap the posts. If you prefer it to be flush with the posts, or if the posts are less than 4 by 4, you can use 2 by 4 stock.

Cut sections of handrail to length. On the stair sections carefully mark the angle needed for the rail to run parallel to the stringers. It is best to span each run with a single piece; if you must make joints, be sure that they occur over a post. On the underside of the rail, cut a groove 1½ inches wide and ⅜ inch deep. Position the rail, making sure that the posts are plumb and that the tenons fit into the groove. Attach the rail to the posts with 12d galvanized casing nails. Toenail the posts to the underside of the rail.

For the lower rails, cut lengths of 2 by 4 to fit between the posts. Make straight cuts on the pieces that form the deck rail and angle cuts on the pieces between the newel and the top post.

Balusters

Measure and cut the balusters to length. Butt-cut the ends for the deck rail sections; angle-cut the ends for the stair rail sections.

It is easier to assemble balusters in sections than to nail them in place individually. Cut pieces of 1½-inch lath to the same lengths as the lower rails. Lay out the pieces of lath and lower rails on the ground and space the balusters between them. Facenail the balusters in place. Lift the assembled sections into position, making sure that the lath strip fits

snugly into the groove on the underside of the handrail. Use parallel clamps on the posts to hold the sections in place while you toenail through the lower rail into the posts.

In another style there is no lower rail and the handrail is turned on edge. The balusters are cut to length with 60-degree angle cuts on top, then fastened to the rim joist with nails or small bolts and to the side of the handrail with nails. The 4 by 4 posts are fastened in the manner described above. The handrail is attached at the proper height—36 inches from top to deck—with the joints positioned at the posts.

Still another style uses horizontal rails to fill the space between the deck and the handrail. The rails are usually 2 by 4s installed at intervals of 6 inches or less and toenailed to the posts at each end.

FINISHING THE INTERIOR

When you have completed the projects in this chapter—putting up ceilings and walls; installing closets, cabinets, and shelves; and adding interior casings and trim—you will be ready to decorate and move into your finished home.

Before starting work on the interior, take a careful look around. Now is the time to make any changes. Try to imagine each room furnished, and foresee possible problems. Where will the bed go? Have you planned outlets for lamps beside it? Will the closet doors clear it? Is there enough storage space?

Although you should have made all the decisions concerning the floor plan before you started to build, you may have had a change of heart, or your requirements may be different now. Decide whether each room is the size and shape you want. Don't change them too hastily—spaces are deceptive when defined only with framing—but even moving a nonbearing wall is not difficult at this stage.

Although there is still a lot of work and mess ahead of you, the excitement of seeing your new home take shape will spur you on.

Finely crafted trim details, such as gracious moldings and small-paned windows, mark the attention of a careful, patient finish carpenter.

SEQUENCE OF ACTIVITIES

As with exterior finish carpentry, there are many materials and techniques you can choose from to finish the interior of your home. Now that the exterior is weatherproof, you can take a well-earned breather and make these decisions at your leisure.

Interior finish work can proceed once the heating, plumbing, wiring, and insulation have been installed.

As you reach each succeeding phase of a house-building project, you must pay more and more attention to detail. This is because the visibility of the work is greater. Your task, then, for this phase of the project is to bring to the job site the appropriate frame of mind and to proceed in the knowledge that you and others will be viewing your handiwork for a long time. This phase represents the culmination of all the skills and experience you have developed over the course of the project. By now you will have gained a certain measure of confidence that you can draw on to get the work done.

Where you choose to do each job and how you set up your work station will affect your efficiency and the quality of the end product. Before starting a given task, visualize the work to be done, the size and nature of the materials you will be handling, and the physical movements required. Once you grasp the whole picture, you can choreograph the activities efficiently.

Remember the underlying principle of all carpentry, which is especially important in the finishing phase: Take measurements twice and cut once. This means that before making any cut, you double-check your measurement. It will undoubtedly save you time, money, and aggravation in the long run. Establish this habit at the beginning; you will soon understand why it pays.

Another technique essential to successful finish work is to install the materials so that they give the best appearance possible, even though there may be flaws or defects in the surrounding materials. Say, for instance, that when installing molding, you find that the walls are not square and you cannot correct this flaw completely. You may have to compensate by making cuts that are not perfectly true and joining pieces together in such a way as to camouflage the connection. This is best accomplished by imagining what the eye will perceive when the work is finished. It is perfectly valid and acceptable to compensate for flaws; to do so skillfully marks your achievement as a finish carpenter.

Remember to get help when you need it. Holding up a long trim piece while trying to nail it in place is not only awkward but also potentially hazardous. A second pair of hands can make the job proceed faster and more safely.

The tools you will need for each of the activities described in this chapter will be discussed in the appropriate sections. Refer to the chapter "Gaining the Skills" for tips on using them.

The general rule for interior finish carpentry is to work from the top down. Cover the ceilings first and then the walls. After that the usual order is to hang the cabinets, construct the interior stairs and railings, hang the shelves, install the door and window casings, put in the wainscoting, install the baseboards and other moldings, and finally build and install the fireplace mantel. In most instances, if you do these jobs out of order, you will have to do some of them twice.

Correct any flaws before you start each activity. This is always advisable; often it is the only way to achieve a fine finish. The flaws requiring remedy are discussed in the appropriate sections following.

It's time to get started. Read each section carefully, follow the directions, and know that you have prepared yourself well for the jobs at hand.

Taping wallboard and installing baseboard are two projects you'll be involved in when finishing the interior of your home.

CEILINGS

The first task in interior finish carpentry is to install the ceiling material. Not only is it a good idea to get this awkward job over with, but it is always better to finish a room by starting at the top and working down.

From the Top Down

There are two main reasons for starting with the ceiling when finishing a room.
• You can get a tight fit between the ceiling and the walls, and later, between the walls and the floor.
• You should always try to install the most visible surfaces last, when they are least likely to be damaged. Dropping a hammer or stepping on spilled nails is almost guaranteed to leave marks on a newly surfaced floor unless it has been very carefully protected.

Lighting

Before you hang the finish ceiling, make all decisions regarding overhead lighting. If you plan to install either a flush-mounted or a pendant fixture, attach an appropriate fixture support to the ceiling box. If your scheme includes recessed spotlights or floodlights, these must be installed before the ceiling is hung. In either case, mark and cut out holes in the ceiling panels before you attach them. Work carefully; although the edges of the holes will be hidden under a cover plate or trim piece, there is not much room for error.

Play It Safe

Wear safety goggles. It is uncomfortable enough working above your head without running the risk of getting dust or shavings in your eyes. Wear a tool belt, too. Balancing tools on top of a ladder can be dangerous, and it is certainly a nuisance when they fall.

Scaffolding

When you're on a ladder, don't try to save time by stretching beyond the area that you can easily reach. Coming down and repositioning the ladder takes a lot less time than waiting for broken bones to mend. If possible, work from scaffolding. You can rent small units that fold up, are adjustable, and have locking casters. If scaffolding is unavailable, erect a simple version by placing a board between two stepladders. Make certain that neither the ladders nor the board can slip.

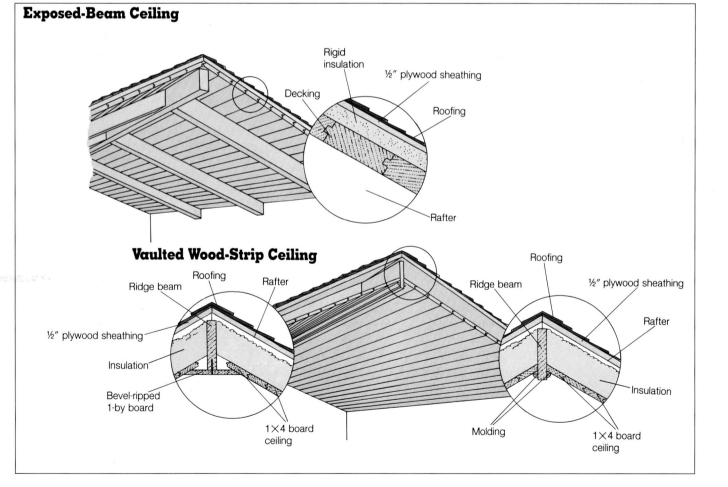

Exposed-Beam Ceiling

Rigid insulation · Decking · ½" plywood sheathing · Roofing · Rafter

Vaulted Wood-Strip Ceiling

Roofing · Rafter · Ridge beam · ½" plywood sheathing · Rafter · Roofing · Ridge beam · ½" plywood sheathing · Insulation · Bevel-ripped 1-by board · 1×4 board ceiling · Molding · Insulation · 1×4 board ceiling

Exposed-Beam Ceiling

In some homes the decking for the roof is also the ceiling for the room below; the rafters and joists (or beams) are exposed from within. With this type of ceiling, use rigid insulation and ⅜-inch plywood sheathing on top of the decking, and then apply the finish roof.

Use decking that is 2 inches thick (nominally). Consider using tongue-and-groove softwood flooring in a C or D grade for the decking. It is available up to 1⁵⁄₁₆ inches thick and 1¾ to 5⁷⁄₁₆ inches wide.

Start the layout for the decking on the upper edge of the rafters, so that the horizontal decking joints at the top of the ridge are parallel to the ridge beam. Starting at the ridge measure down the rafters at each end of the roof the distance necessary to completely cover the roof, and make a mark at this point. Stretch a chalk line from end rafter to end rafter at this mark. Snap the line across all the rafters. This is the true starting point for installing the decking.

Align the first piece of decking with the snapped line. Facenail it with two 16-penny (16d) hot-dipped galvanized nails at each rafter. Complete the first course of decking in the same way. Be sure to center the joints over the rafters. Proceed with the next course of decking, this time using one face nail and one blind nail driven down diagonally through the tongue of the decking into the rafter. This drives the groove of the piece of decking tightly against the tongue of the previous piece, giving it a finished look.

As you install the succeeding courses of decking, take periodic measurements to make sure that they are still parallel to the ridge. You will probably find that the distance is increasing at one or more of the rafters. If this happens, allow the seams to open slightly over the next few courses where the distance is shortest. Do this until you regain a line parallel to the ridge.

You will undoubtedly fall into a comfortable routine, checking every four or five courses to ensure consistency. Try to keep the seams as far as possible from the walls and ridge, to minimize the effect of nonparallel lines. This may require that the starter piece be ripped to the dimension that allows for the maximum distance between wall and seam.

Vaulted Wood-Strip Ceiling

With this type of ceiling, the wood strips are nailed to the bottom of the rafters, unless local codes require a layer of wallboard under the rafters. Batt insulation can be installed between the strips and the roof sheathing. To achieve a tight fit, tongue-and-groove strips are better than straight-cut boards.

A wood-strip ceiling is generally installed with the strips running horizontally. Place the first course (groove side down) so that the bottom edge butts up to the wall. As with the installation of roof decking described above, the starter course of wood strip should be positioned to allow for parallel seam lines as the ceiling reaches the ridge beam. You

may have to rip the starter piece at an angle to achieve this result, because the wall and the ridge beam may not be parallel. Plan carefully so that the last board you install against the ridge is as close to full width as possible.

Nail the starter piece in place and continue to the peak. The best appearance is achieved when wood-strip ceiling material is blind-nailed, and no face nailing is done. This means that only one nail is used for each course of wood strip, but this is ordinarily sufficient for 1-by material. Measure frequently and make small adjustments so that the final course is parallel to the ridge beam. Place insulation between the rafters as you proceed. A ridge beam protruding into the room can be edged with strips of molding, or it can serve as a nailing board for a piece of bevel-ripped 1-by stock.

When 1-by material is used, the rafters should be spaced no wider than 24 inches on center for best appearance.

Crisscrossed-Beam Ceiling

Ornate beamed ceilings can be created using decorative trim installed beneath a standard ceiling of wallboard or wood paneling. Before starting the actual installation, experiment with various combinations of moldings and dimensioned lumber to create a pleasing design. Work out a pattern that attaches easily to standard framing lumber (2 by 2, 2 by 4, and 4 by 4 are the most commonly used). See pages 108 and 109 for examples.

The first step is to attach a grid of framing members to the

ceiling to support the pieces of decorative molding. The size of the framing members can vary depending on the scale of the room. For smaller rooms use 2 by 2s or 2 by 4s. Run the first pieces full length across the ceiling, perpendicular to the ceiling joists and spaced 3 to 4 feet apart. Snap chalk lines on the ceiling to keep the framing straight. Secure the framing members where they intersect each ceiling joist with a self-tapping wallboard screw or a lag screw. The screw should penetrate the ceiling joist at least 1 inch. Countersink the heads of the lag screws.

When all the full-length members are in place, cut and install identical framing pieces between them to create a crisscross grid. Apply a bead of construction adhesive to the top of each crosspiece. Then hold it in place against the ceiling and either toenail or screw each end to the full-length framing member.

For larger rooms with long spans or ones that require massive beams, you can make lightweight hollow box beams out of 2 by 4s and plywood. Attach the upper 2 by 4 members first, as described above. Then, to complete the beams and make them deeper, fabricate continuous U-shaped channels the same length as each ceiling member, using 2 by 4s with plywood glued and nailed to the sides. Nail each channel to the corresponding grid member on the ceiling.

Once the framework grid is in place, attach the decorative trim pieces to the sides and bottom of the beams.

WALLBOARD CEILINGS AND WALLS

The most widely used covering for interior walls and ceilings is wallboard. It has almost entirely replaced lath and plaster in general residential applications because it has the properties of plaster and many other advantages as well.

Properties of Wallboard

You may recognize wallboard by one of its other names—drywall, plasterboard, gypboard, or Sheetrock. The gypsum core used in wallboard panels is very similar to plaster (it lacks sand), but it has been mixed at the factory and formed into sheets that are covered with special paper on each side. Here are some of its advantages.
• The sheets are inexpensive and easy to cut.
• The sheet form enables you to obtain flat wall surfaces without acquiring the specialized skills of a plasterer.
• The gypsum compound in wallboard retains 20 percent water, which makes the wallboard fire resistant.
• Manufactured sizes conform to standard wall heights.

Selecting Wallboard

Wallboard usually comes in 4 by 8 panels, although longer panels are sometimes available. The standard thicknesses are ¼ inch, ⅜ inch, ½ inch, and ⅝ inch.
• The ½-inch sheet is the standard panel for residential construction. It combines ease of handling with good impact resistance. A 4 by 8 sheet of

½-inch wallboard weighs 58 pounds—light enough for one person to handle.
• The ⅝-inch sheet is often used for truss ceilings where the truss spacing is 24 inches on center. It is also used on common walls between a house and an attached garage, for example, for greater fire protection.
• The ¼-inch sheet is used primarily for resurfacing existing walls. Because it has little impact resistance, it must be solidly supported.
• The ⅜-inch sheet can be used for resurfacing, but it is more often hung in a double layer to make ¾-inch walls. The sound-insulating properties of a double panel make it a good choice for recreation rooms.
• Special ½-inch wallboard is manufactured for use in high-humidity areas, such as bathrooms and laundry rooms. This type of wallboard is identified by the light green or blue cover paper, which is moisture resistant. In addition, the core is made of a moisture-resistant gypsum compound.

Insulating wallboard is similar to regular wallboard except that it has a foil coating on one side. To obtain the benefit, you must leave a ¾-inch air space between the foil and any other insulation. The foil also acts as a vapor barrier.

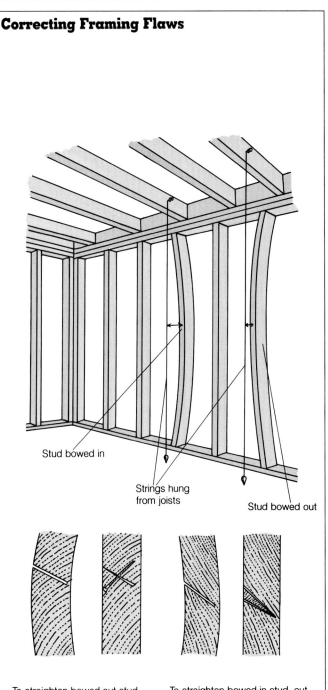

Correcting Framing Flaws

Stud bowed in

Strings hung from joists

Stud bowed out

To straighten bowed-out stud, cut diagonal kerf with circular saw, reciprocating saw, or handsaw. Drive 2½" wallboard screw on opposite diagonal to pull kerf closed and straighten stud.

To straighten bowed-in stud, cut diagonal kerf; then drive sufficient number of shims into cut to straighten stud. Nail 3"-wide strip of plywood to long face of stud for stability.

Wallboard is available with a decorative surface laminated to one side. This surface, usually vinyl, comes in colors, patterns, and simulated wood grain or marble. Consider this for a child's room, where it is often necessary to remove a future Picasso's handiwork from the walls.

Be aware that installing wallboard, although not difficult, is extremely messy, arduous, and time-consuming for the amateur. If the budget allows, call in the pros. You will be amazed at how quickly and seemingly easily they get the job done.

Preparing for Installation

Hanging wallboard is much easier if the joists and studs are even and square. Check with a string nailed to the member in question. If you find studs that bulge inward or outward more than about ⅛ inch, correct the problem before proceeding. If a stud is bulging out, straighten it by making a diagonal handsaw cut about three quarters of the way through the stud; then drive a screw through the cut to squeeze it together. A bulging stud may also be straightened by shaving or planing. If a stud is curved inward, make the same cut; drive in enough shims to straighten the stud; then nail a 3-inch piece of plywood scrap alongside the stud for stability. See illustration on page 67.

Other flaws and oversights should be corrected before the wallboard is hung. Check to see that all electrical outlet boxes are extended away from the

stud or ceiling joist at the proper distance to receive the wallboard. Finally, be sure to provide a backing wherever the wallboard is to be fastened.

To prepare for installation remove any moldings attached to the window frames. Bring the wallboard into the room and stack it in the middle of the floor. If you lean it against a wall, you run the risk of cracking or warping the panels and damaging the edges.

Studs, plumbing, and electrical conduits determine where the wallboard can be nailed. You want to hit the studs, not the conduits or the plumbing. Before putting up the wallboard, remember to attach protection plates to studs

drilled for plumbing and wiring; nails won't penetrate the protection plates.

So you'll know where to nail the ceiling wallboard once it covers the joists, mark the location of the joists on the plates. When the ceiling wallboard is in place, mark on it the location of the studs, so you'll know where to nail the wallboard for the walls. See illustration. Tack the wallboard adjacent to the joist and stud marks. Then snap a chalk line as a guide for nailing.

When soundproofing is required between living levels in a multistory dwelling, you can install a sheet-metal strip, called resilient channel, on the ceiling of the lower level, to which a second layer of wallboard is attached. This reduces the sound transmission between levels. See illustration on page 70, right.

Measuring and Laying Out Wallboard

When more than one measurement is involved in a sequence, take progressive readings with a steel tape in one position, rather than moving the tape after each reading. This reduces cumulative error.

To take progressive readings lay a panel of wallboard on sawhorses in the same position as that in which it will be installed. Touch the tip of the tape measure to a ceiling-wall corner or to the edge of the adjacent piece of wallboard. Extend the tape to the first edge of any cutout that you come to, such as an electrical outlet box, a recessed light fixture, a window or door frame, or a

Marking Joists and Studs

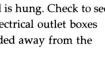

1. Mark location of ceiling joists on plates to indicate where to nail when wallboard covers joists

2. Mark location of studs on ceiling covering to indicate where to nail when wallboard covers studs

wall opening. Record this dimension on a scrap of wallboard on which you have first drawn the entire schematic of cutouts for this panel. Then extend the tape to the other side of the cutout and record this dimension on the schematic. Measure any other cutouts necessary to complete the panel in one direction. Then take perpendicular measurements: Touch the tip of the tape to the wall (or to the ceiling if you're measuring a wall panel) or the adjacent piece of wallboard, then follow the same procedure. See illustration at right.

Make the actual cutouts about ¼ inch larger all around than the dimensions on the schematic. This makes it easier to install the panel. The exception is cutouts for electrical boxes, which should be within ⅛ inch or less of the actual size of the box.

Cutting Wallboard

Cut sheets of wallboard by scoring the top (finish) surface with a utility knife. Draw a line with a pencil first or snap a chalk line on the face of the sheet. Use a T square (the 4-foot size is the handiest) to ensure that the line is straight. Now bend the board backward. If it does not break easily, bend it over a 2 by 4 or use your knee. After the wallboard snaps, cut the back surface with the utility knife. If the break is not clean and gypsum protrudes beyond the edge of the paper, use a rasp to remove the excess.

Use a wallboard saw to cut holes or irregular shapes in the panels. This pointed saw, which has a sturdy 6-inch blade and five teeth per inch, can poke right through a panel to start a cut, and the coarse teeth will not clog up. See illustration below.

Measuring and Marking Wallboard

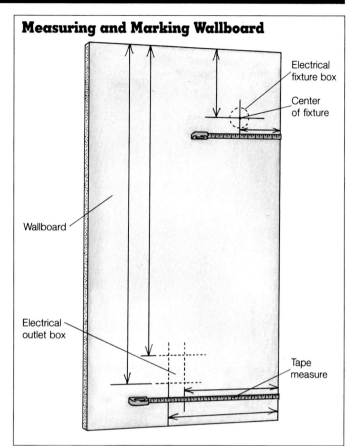

Electrical fixture box

Center of fixture

Wallboard

Electrical outlet box

Tape measure

Wallboard Tools

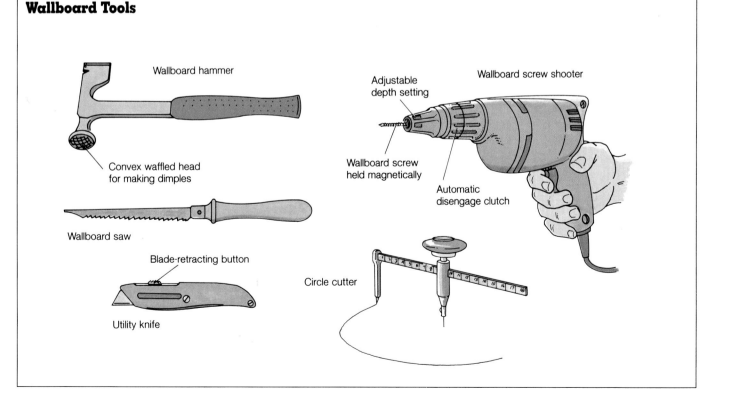

Wallboard hammer

Convex waffled head for making dimples

Wallboard saw

Blade-retracting button

Utility knife

Adjustable depth setting

Wallboard screw shooter

Wallboard screw held magnetically

Automatic disengage clutch

Circle cutter

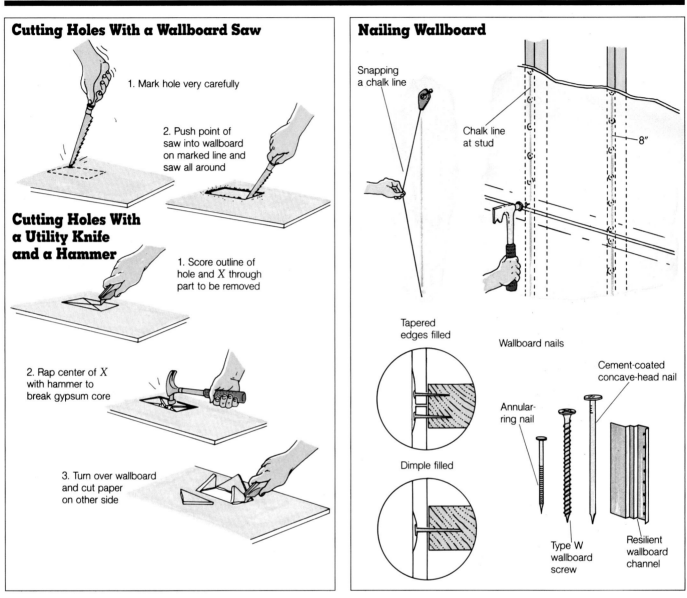

Cutting Holes With a Wallboard Saw

1. Mark hole very carefully

2. Push point of saw into wallboard on marked line and saw all around

Cutting Holes With a Utility Knife and a Hammer

1. Score outline of hole and X through part to be removed

2. Rap center of X with hammer to break gypsum core

3. Turn over wallboard and cut paper on other side

Nailing Wallboard

Snapping a chalk line

Chalk line at stud

8"

Tapered edges filled

Wallboard nails

Dimple filled

Cement-coated concave-head nail

Annular-ring nail

Type W wallboard screw

Resilient wallboard channel

An adjustable compasslike device called a circle cutter scores accurate circles. It has a ¾-inch pin at the point. Push the pin through the front of the wallboard and score the edge of the circle. Use the same hole to score another circle on the back of the wallboard. Punch out the circle. See illustration on page 69, bottom.

Be sure to measure each panel carefully. Plot the cuts in pencil on the surface of the board and recheck the measurements before you break the surface.

If you have some scrap wallboard to practice on, try the method that the pros use to make rectangular cuts—it is fast once you get the knack. Pencil the cuts onto the board and score them with a utility knife as described above. Score an X through the area to be cut and tap the center with a hammer. This loosens four wedge-shaped pieces, which fall free when you cut the back cover paper. See illustration above left.

Attaching Wallboard

Wallboard may be nailed, screwed, or glued to the studs. Whichever method you use, the panels should fit snugly against each other. Do not economize by using cut pieces of wallboard. The material is cheap, and the joints are not as neat when neither butted panel has a tapered edge.

Nailing Wallboard

The most common method of attaching wallboard is nailing. Use the annular-ring nails designed especially for this purpose; the rings should prevent the nails from popping out. See illustration above right. Choose a nail long enough to penetrate the framing ¾ inch to 1 inch after passing through the wallboard.

Let the framing reach its stabilized moisture content before nailing into it. Wood shrinks as it dries, which makes the nails pop out. If possible, close the doors and windows and keep the room at about 72° F for at least four days, preferably two weeks, before you install the wallboard.

When attaching the ceiling panels, space the nails 7 inches apart along each joist and no less than ⅜ inch from the edge of a panel. Attach the wall panels with nails spaced 8 inches apart along each stud. For a

handy nail-spacing guide, affix pieces of tape to your hammer handle 7 inches and 8 inches from the head.

Be careful not to break the cover paper of the wallboard when you drive in the nails. Using a special wallboard hammer will reduce the risk of damaging the surface. The checked face of the hammerhead is bell shaped to seat the nail head below the surface. See illustration on page 69, bottom.

Screwing Wallboard

Wallboard can also be attached with screws. This method is becoming popular; however, you will need a drill with a clutch, which costs between $90 and $130. The special bit can be bought at most home-improvement centers for about $1. For small jobs it may be more economical to rent the tool, but be realistic about how long the job will take.

The 1¼-inch Type W screws are stronger than nails. See illustration on page 70, right. You can space them up to 12 inches apart on the ceiling and up to 16 inches apart on a wall, but not closer than ⅜ inch to the edge of the panel. The screws are driven by a Phillips screwdriver bit in a drill with an automatic disengage, which activates just as you countersink the screw head.

Unlike nails, screws do not require a fine touch. Just keep an even, solid pressure on the drill. Don't let the bit jump the screw slots or you will have a very messy hole.

Gluing Wallboard

Wallboard held to the studs by adhesive makes a stronger wall and one that absorbs more sound. Using adhesive also eliminates nail holes—and the job of filling them. Predecorated panels look better glued, even though matching nails are usually available.

This method is well suited to small jobs, on which you can use 1-quart cartridges of adhesive. Large jobs are done with a refillable applicator and adhesive in 5-gallon cans.

Hold the applicator at a 45-degree angle to the framing member and apply a ⅜-inch-wide bead of adhesive. Use a zigzag pattern on members where two panels meet. See illustration.

After you have applied the adhesive, lift the panel into position and press it firmly against the beads of glue. Nail or screw the outer edges only

Gluing Wallboard

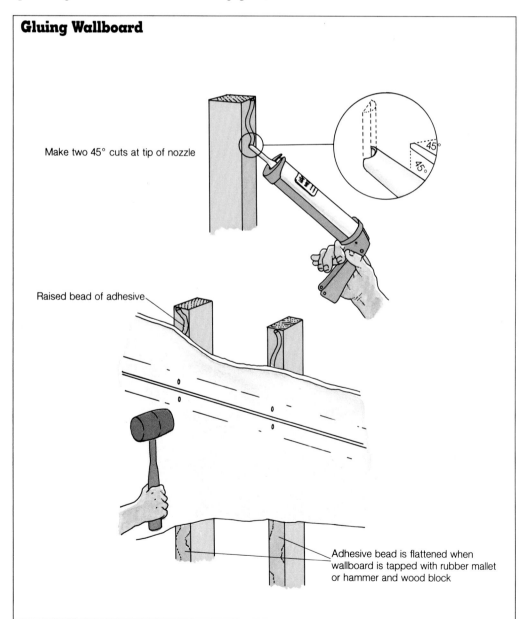

Make two 45° cuts at tip of nozzle

Raised bead of adhesive

Adhesive bead is flattened when wallboard is tapped with rubber mallet or hammer and wood block

Supporting a Ceiling Panel

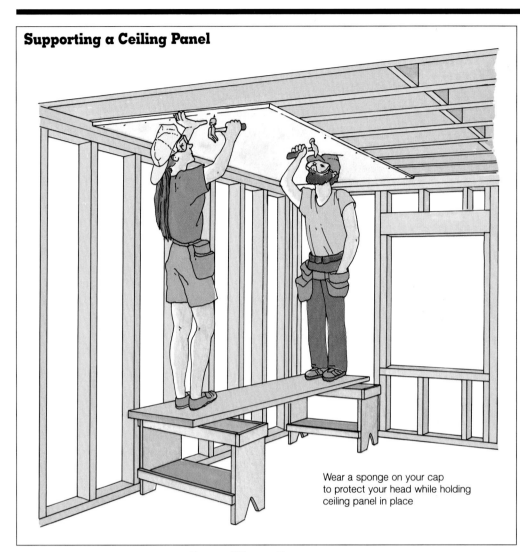

Wear a sponge on your cap
to protect your head while holding
ceiling panel in place

or tap with a rubber mallet. To ensure contact and to spread the adhesive, hold a 2 by 4 protection block against the surface and strike the glue lines with a hammer.

On predecorated panels overlap the extra surface material or attach matching battens over the joints.

Installing the Ceiling

It is best to have help when you install the ceiling (see illustration). However, you can do it alone if necessary, using a T-brace or a rented wallboard jack. A T-brace is simply a long 2 by 4 with a crosspiece nailed at the top. The long upright must be slightly longer than the floor-to-ceiling distance so that the T-brace can be jammed up under a piece of wallboard

to hold one end in position while you nail the other. To cushion your head for holding wallboard against the ceiling as you nail it, wear a hard hat or a cap with a sponge under it.

A jack is much easier to use. You place a sheet of wallboard on it, then crank the jack so

that it lifts the wallboard up to the ceiling and holds it there. The jack is on wheels so that you can roll it around to position the wallboard perfectly. Start by positioning a full panel in one corner. Attach the panel to the joists, using the method of your choice. Cut the last panel in each row ¼ inch short, to provide clearance at the end. If the walls are going to be finished with wallboard, nail no closer than 7 inches to the edge of a ceiling panel; the butting panel will tighten the joint. Complete the first row, placing the panels end to end. Position the joints on the joists, as close as possible to the center of the joists. A dozen or so fasteners will hold each panel in place until the remaining ceiling panels are installed, at which time you can finish fastening all of them. Cut the first panel of the next row in half, since staggering the joints results in a finer job.

When you come to a panel that needs a cutout—for a light fixture or a trapdoor to the attic, for example—transfer the measurements from the ceiling to the wallboard before raising the panel. (See Measuring and Laying Out Wallboard, page 68.) Pencil the cut lines onto the face of the panel so that the opening will be no larger than necessary. Recheck your measurements before you cut.

If you are covering the walls with wallboard, put these panels up before taping and filling the ceiling.

Foot Fulcrums

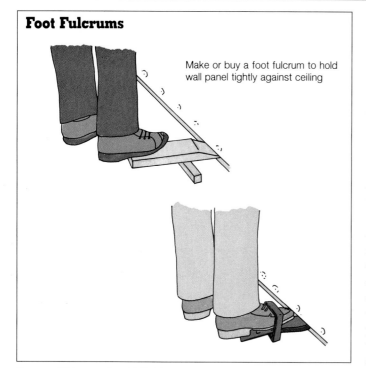

Make or buy a foot fulcrum to hold wall panel tightly against ceiling

Installing the Walls

The materials and techniques used to cover walls are basically the same as those used for ceilings. Since the studs run vertically, the preferred position for the panels is horizontal. It is acceptable—and in fact faster—to run them vertically, but this way the joints are more likely to show as the structure settles. Fit each panel snugly against the ceiling; use wedges or a foot fulcrum (see illustration) to help you to get a tight fit. A gap of ½ inch to ¾ inch at the bottom is acceptable—it will be covered later by the baseboard.

Starting in one corner slide the panel up against the ceiling and attach it with nails, screws, or glue, as described on pages 70 to 72. If you're placing the panels horizontally, complete the upper row around the room. Cut out openings as

accurately as you can; plates will cover the holes you make for electrical outlets and switches, but they don't allow much room for error. Openings for doors and windows are less critical, because the gaps will be covered by molding. Avoid joints at the corners of doors and windows, since cracks are more likely to appear at these locations.

The second of the two panels forming an inside corner butts up to and holds the first panel against the framing. For this reason you don't need to nail or screw the first panel along the butted edge. The panels forming an outside corner lap must be capped with a metal corner beading to protect the edge. The beading is covered later with joint compound.

Taping and Filling the Joints

Whether the wallboard is attached with nails, screws, or glue, you have to hide the joints and fasteners. Vinyl-covered predecorated wallboard may have a flap to cover the joint, but standard wallboard must be taped and filled, a process sometimes referred to as mudding.

You need 4-inch, 6-inch, and 10-inch putty knives, a corner knife, paper tape, and joint compound. You can buy powder and mix your own joint compound following the manufacturer's directions, or buy it premixed in containers holding up to 5 gallons. If you are using a large container of compound, scoop a small amount into a tray and work from this. Clean out the tray often, because dust and dried-out compound make it difficult to get a smooth surface.

Start by spreading a quantity of compound into a joint with a 4-inch knife. Lay the tape on the wet compound and embed it smoothly. (Some people find that wetting the tape before pressing it into place makes application easier.) Apply more joint compound over the tape with the 6-inch knife, feathering the edges. Repeat this procedure for all the joints. Fill all nail dimples—you don't need tape here. Allow the compound to dry; then sand lightly before applying the next coat. See illustration on page 74.

An alternative to paper tape is a 2-inch-wide strip of fiberglass mesh that has a light adhesive on one side. This strip

can be applied to the joint prior to mudding; the joint compound penetrates through the openings in the mesh to the surface of the wallboard, speeding up the drying process.

Apply a second, wider coat with a 6-inch knife. Feather the edges, getting them as smooth as you can, and sand lightly when dry. (You can get a good finish and make less mess by smoothing the compound with a damp sponge.) Two coats are sufficient if you are going to apply texture compound. If you are going to paint or paper the walls or if you require a smooth surface for some other reason, apply a third coat with a 10-inch knife.

Finish inside corners and wall-ceiling joints in the same way. Apply the compound to the corner, smoothing it with a corner knife. Fold sections of tape lengthwise, place them on the wet compound, and use the corner knife to press them into place. Apply another coat over the tape and smooth it with the knife. Let it dry, sand lightly, and then apply a second coat.

On outside corners the metal beading takes the place of tape. Apply two or more coats of compound, letting it dry and sanding between coats.

Note: There are many ways to texture wallboard to make it look like plaster, but they all entail applying compound over the entire surface with a sponge, roller, or trowel. Experiment on scraps before doing this, or call in a wallboard professional.

Taping and Filling Joints and Dimples

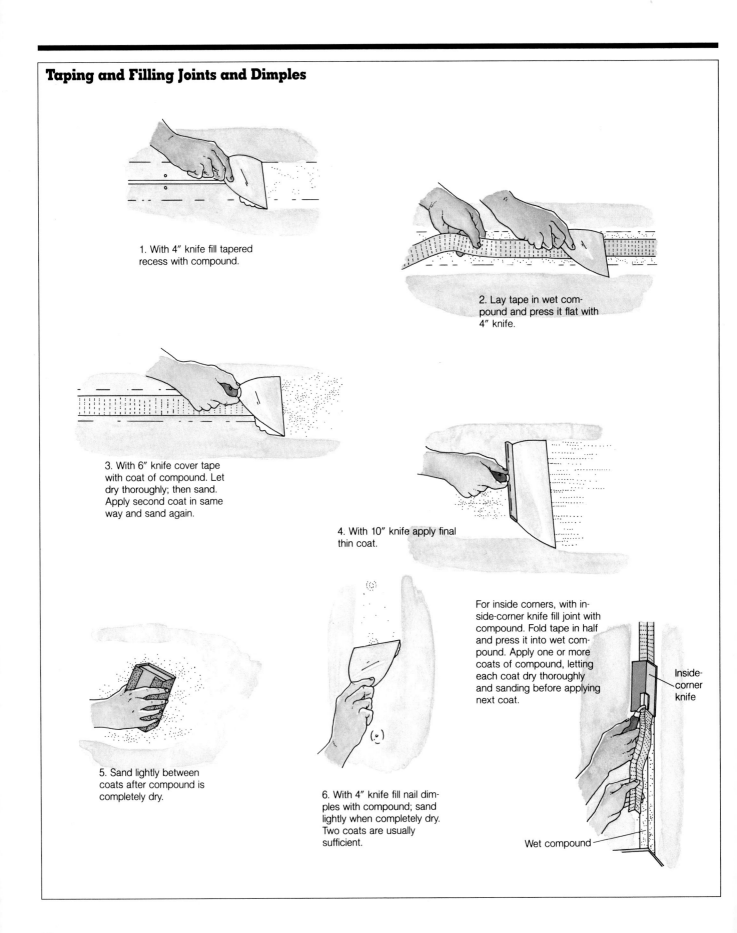

1. With 4″ knife fill tapered recess with compound.

2. Lay tape in wet compound and press it flat with 4″ knife.

3. With 6″ knife cover tape with coat of compound. Let dry thoroughly; then sand. Apply second coat in same way and sand again.

4. With 10″ knife apply final thin coat.

5. Sand lightly between coats after compound is completely dry.

6. With 4″ knife fill nail dimples with compound; sand lightly when completely dry. Two coats are usually sufficient.

For inside corners, with inside-corner knife fill joint with compound. Fold tape in half and press it into wet compound. Apply one or more coats of compound, letting each coat dry thoroughly and sanding before applying next coat.

Inside-corner knife

Wet compound

WALL PANELING

Even if you don't use wood wallcoverings throughout the house, there are rooms that look particularly good decorated this way—the den or library, for example. A wide selection of panels is available; some are routed to look like individual boards.

Sheet Paneling

This type of paneling is actually ¼-inch plywood with a surface veneer in a selection of hardwoods, softwoods, textures, solids, simulated marble, and brick—the choice and the price range are large. You can even get wallpaper veneer over a ⅛-inch plywood backing.

The 4 by 8 sheet is standard, but 9-foot and 10-foot lengths are also available. The sheets should always be applied vertically to avoid unsightly joints, so use the long ones if you have high ceilings.

Paneling can be installed over studs and over almost any existing wall surface, even concrete.

Over Studs

You can make the wall more solid and increase sound insulation by first covering the studs with ⅜-inch or ½-inch wallboard. See illustration. There is no need to tape and fill, but you should stagger the wallboard and paneling joints.

Over Concrete or Concrete Block

Apply a coat of asphalt mastic (with or without plastic film over it) as a vapor barrier. Using a nailing gun (see page 41) or hand-driven concrete nails, attach horizontal 1 by 2 furring strips every 16 inches. Attach vertical furring blocks between the horizontal strips at 48-inch intervals. Lay out the paneling so that the joints fall over these vertical blocks.

Once the support system is in place, attach the paneling with either nails or adhesive. You can buy nails with heads to match the color of the paneling or the darker grooves. You can also use finishing nails and cover the heads with a special putty available in a convenient crayonlike stick.

Adhesives come in easy-to-use cartridges. Adhesives are not all the same; follow the manufacturer's instructions. You must cut, fit, and mark the exact position of each panel before you apply the adhesive. Once the glue is on, it's too late to make adjustments.

Installing Sheet Paneling

When you use a circular power saw to cut paneling, you must cut with the face of the panel down so that any splintering occurs on the backside. A plywood blade, which is designed to reduce splintering, makes for a neater job. If you use a handsaw or a table saw, be sure to cut the paneling face up.

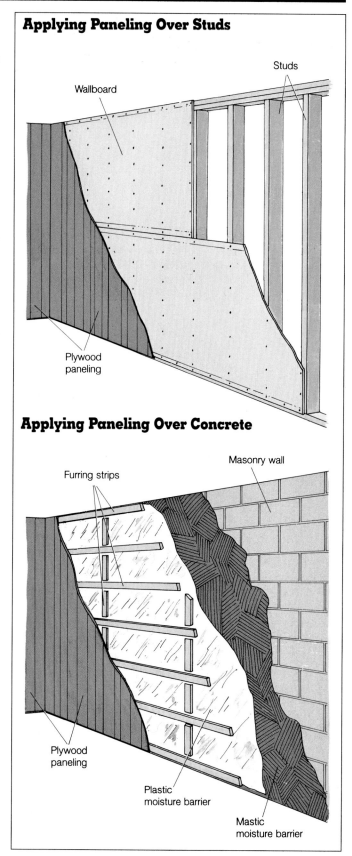

Applying Paneling Over Studs

Wallboard

Studs

Plywood paneling

Applying Paneling Over Concrete

Furring strips

Masonry wall

Plywood paneling

Plastic moisture barrier

Mastic moisture barrier

Fitting an Irregular Edge

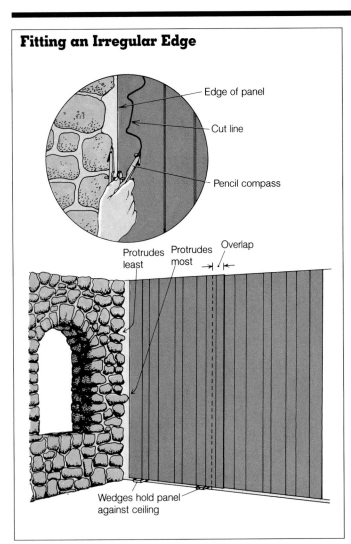

Start by placing a full sheet of paneling in one corner and continue around the room. Make sure that the first panel is plumb—if it is not, the entire installation will be crooked. Gaps at the top and bottom can be covered by molding. Mark cutouts as you come to them. Check your measurements and then cut, using a compass saw or a saber saw.

Irregular shapes can be traced directly onto the panel with a compass and pencil. Place the panel against the irregular surface. Adjust the compass so that the span equals the amount that this panel overlaps the one next to it. If this is a first panel, butt it against the point that protrudes the most and set the compass for the distance between the edge of the panel and the point that protrudes the least. For the final panel, set the compass to the amount of overlap. In either case, mark the panel and cut with a saber saw or a compass saw. See illustration.

Board Paneling

A more traditional way to obtain wood-finished walls is to cover them with paneling boards. These come in a variety of species, grades, and mill patterns, with softwoods dominating the list. If you want wormy chestnut or cherry, consider laminated veneer panels rather than board paneling; hardwood boards are very expensive. Paneling boards are commonly available in 4-inch to 12-inch widths and with tongue-and-groove or straight-cut sides.

Board paneling is usually applied vertically. First, cover the studs with wallboard. Then attach 1 by 2 furring strips horizontally, nailing them to the studs. If you are surfacing a smoothly sheathed wall, you can glue the boards with a panel adhesive. In this case, furring strips will not be needed.

With tongue-and-groove boards, drive 6d finishing nails into the V at the base of the tongue at a 45-degree angle and set the heads. See illustration on page 77. The next board clips over the tongue and covers the nail holes.

To keep from ending with a piece that is conspicuously narrower than the rest, you can work back from each corner with whole boards. A narrow board above a door or at a window will be barely noticeable. Keep in mind that board paneling plus furring strips adds up to a thickness at least 1½ inches greater than that of standard wallcoverings. Use thicker door frames or add square molding to build up the edge of standard frames.

Board-paneled walls can be finished in a number of ways. Varnish, shellac, stain, paint, bleach, and antiquing (paint applied and then partially rubbed off with a rag) are some of the options.

Wainscoting

Wainscoting is decorative wood wallcovering, such as paneling or tongue-and-groove boards,

Redwood board paneling covers the walls, ceiling, and skylight well of this room. The tongue-and-groove configuration of the boards allows the nails to be concealed, a technique known as blind-nailing.

Attaching Tongue-And-Groove Paneling

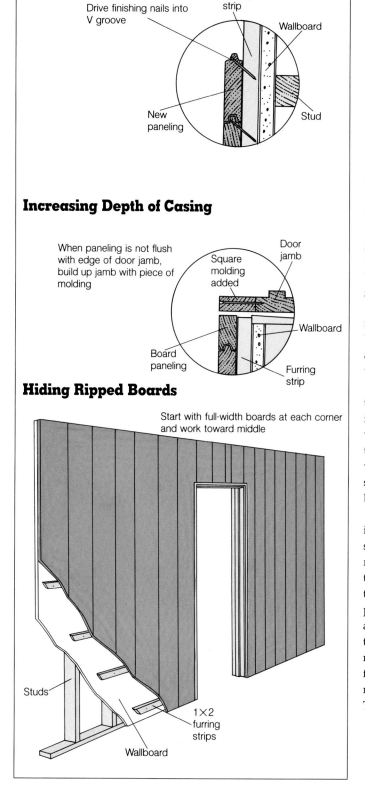

Drive finishing nails into V groove

Furring strip

Wallboard

New paneling

Stud

Increasing Depth of Casing

When paneling is not flush with edge of door jamb, build up jamb with piece of molding

Square molding added

Door jamb

Wallboard

Board paneling

Furring strip

Hiding Ripped Boards

Start with full-width boards at each corner and work toward middle

Studs

1×2 furring strips

Wallboard

that is applied to the lower part of a wall. The paneling can be solid wood (square edged or tongue and groove), veneered plywood, or hardboard. The method of installation differs with the type of wainscoting.

Installing Tongue-And-Groove Wainscoting

Tongue-and-groove boards are installed perpendicular to the floor. Begin the installation by chalking a horizontal line on the wall to indicate the height of the wainscoting. Measure the pieces so that they will stop just short of the floor and cut them all to length ahead of time. Baseboard will cover the gap at the bottom.

Since each piece must be nailed in at least three places, board wainscoting requires a continuous backing. This is usually provided by letting 1 by 4s into the studs horizontally before the wallboard is installed. For remodel jobs where there is no access behind the wallcovering, ½-inch plywood can be installed on the surface of the wall to provide backing for the wainscoting.

If there are outside corners, it's better to start with them, since they are especially prominent and visible. You can miter the mating pieces or square-cut them. In either case, glue these pieces together at the corner and nail them 8 inches on center (nail in both directions for a miter). Hold the corner very firmly so that the pieces do not move away from the wall. Then work your way toward

inside corners and window and door casings, nailing each piece at an angle through the tongue into the backing at about 12 inches on center. (Other than the mitered or square-cut outside corner described above, tongue-and-groove joints should not be glued.)

At inside corners allow a small gap between the piece and the corner. As you prepare to install the mating piece, consider ripping it to a width that will match the reveal on the piece previously installed. This is a refinement that indicates a more thoughtful approach to the job.

At doors and windows take very careful measurements from the top, middle, and bottom of each casing to the piece of wainscoting previously installed. If the measurements are all the same and are less than the width of a full piece, draw a vertical line between the bottom and top marks, allowing a little extra width for adjustment. Cut or plane the piece as necessary to achieve a good fit. If the measurements are different, a line drawn between the top and bottom marks will not align with the middle mark, so draw a vertical line between the top and middle marks, and another between the bottom and middle marks. Cut along these lines to more closely match the contour of the mating piece. Adjust the piece to fit; then facenail it to the backing close to the casing. Set all exposed nail heads. See illustration on page 78.

In very humid climates leave a thin gap beside each piece to allow for expansion and contraction. Use shim material about 1/16 inch thick.

Fitting and Cutting Wainscoting

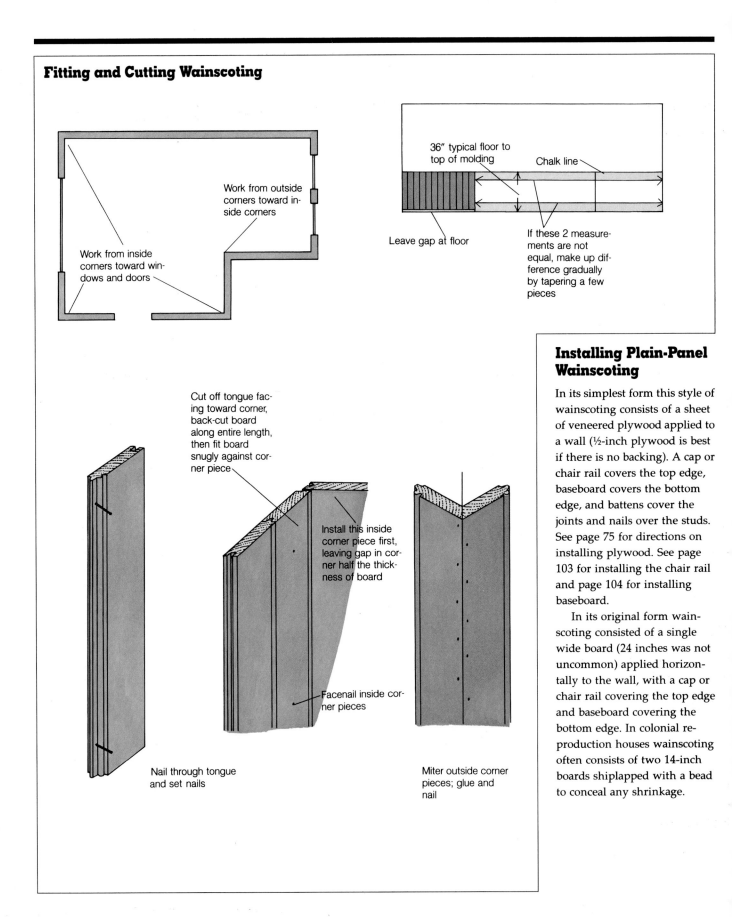

Work from outside corners toward inside corners

Work from inside corners toward windows and doors

36" typical floor to top of molding

Chalk line

Leave gap at floor

If these 2 measurements are not equal, make up difference gradually by tapering a few pieces

Cut off tongue facing toward corner, back-cut board along entire length, then fit board snugly against corner piece

Install this inside corner piece first, leaving gap in corner half the thickness of board

Nail through tongue and set nails

Facenail inside corner pieces

Miter outside corner pieces; glue and nail

Installing Plain-Panel Wainscoting

In its simplest form this style of wainscoting consists of a sheet of veneered plywood applied to a wall (½-inch plywood is best if there is no backing). A cap or chair rail covers the top edge, baseboard covers the bottom edge, and battens cover the joints and nails over the studs. See page 75 for directions on installing plywood. See page 103 for installing the chair rail and page 104 for installing baseboard.

In its original form wainscoting consisted of a single wide board (24 inches was not uncommon) applied horizontally to the wall, with a cap or chair rail covering the top edge and baseboard covering the bottom edge. In colonial reproduction houses wainscoting often consists of two 14-inch boards shiplapped with a bead to conceal any shrinkage.

CLOSETS

The popular prefabricated modular closet units are designed for the most efficient use of space and easy access. They are discussed below, along with traditional, contemporary, and multipurpose closets. Choose the size and type of closet that will provide you with the storage space you need.

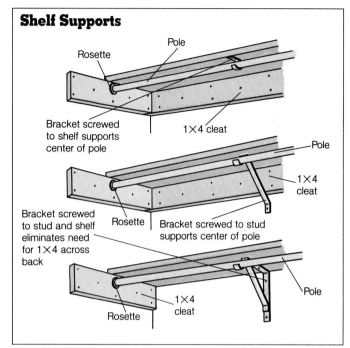

Shelf Supports

Rosette
Pole
Bracket screwed to shelf supports center of pole
1×4 cleat

Pole
1×4 cleat
Bracket screwed to stud and shelf eliminates need for 1×4 across back
Rosette
Bracket screwed to stud supports center of pole

1×4 cleat
Rosette
Pole

Planning Ahead

Adding a closet requires the same rough framing as installing a non-load-bearing wall. The framework must be tied into existing studs and joists, so install closets before applying the finish wall, floor, and ceiling surfaces. If this is not feasible, locate studs and joists by referring to the blueprints of the building, by removing some of the finish material, or by using a stud finder.

Check with the local building department to determine whether you will need a building permit (any new electrical wiring will require one). Then draw detailed plans. Bear in mind that you should allow 12 inches behind and at least 12 inches in front of a closet pole. (Remember to allow for finish wall surfaces.) Position the closet wall at a stud location. If necessary, adjust the size of the closet or toenail an additional stud into the existing wall. Frame the opening to fit the closet doors of your choice. Finally, install the wallcovering and add the shelves, drawers, and poles.

Traditional Closets

A clothes closet needs at least one shelf and a pole. These are usually supported by 1 by 4 cleats fastened to the studs on the side walls and across the back. Allow at least 12 inches behind and in front of the pole. Its top should be 63¼ inches from the floor. Wood poles that span more than 48 inches will need center support. Wood dowel 1¼ inches or 1⅜ inches in diameter is generally used for closet poles, but ¾-inch steel pipe works well and is more rigid.

Measuring for Closet Shelves

See page 91 for detailed information on measuring for closet shelves.

Installing the Parts

First, attach a cleat to the rear wall of the closet, positioning the top edge 2¾ inches above the pole and 66 inches from the floor. Check with a spirit level before nailing or screwing the cleat into the studs (use two nails at each stud). Attach matching side cleats between the rear and front walls. Screw wood or plastic closet pole hangers to the side cleats. Cut the dowel or pipe to length and drop it into the hangers. To

prevent the pole from sagging, purchase any of the many metal supports available and attach it to either the wall or the shelf. See illustration. Set all nail heads.

For the shelf cut a 1-by board to length. (See page 91 for installation procedures.) Finish the front edge with a shaper or a router, or attach a piece of molding with glue and finishing nails.

Contemporary Closets

Efficiency has dictated the design of the contemporary closet. Shelves, drawers, and poles are organized to make the best use of space and to provide easy access. This can be achieved in several ways: by using traditional methods of construction but installing

the parts in a contemporary configuration; by purchasing prefabricated modular units that fit into the available space; or by using a combination of both techniques.

With the traditional method of construction, you begin by creating your own design. Decide how many shelves and dividers you want and the horizontal and vertical dimensions of each. Decide where drawers are to be located and where and how high you want the poles to be.

Start with the side cleats; fasten them to each wall at standard height. Cut and install the shelf (see illustrations on pages 81 and 91). Mark it for vertical dividers. Measure and cut the dividers and install them in their respective positions. Nail through the shelf down into the top end of each divider, using three 6d finishing nails (glue the joint first), and toenail the bottom of each divider to the floor, using three 6d finishing nails on each side. Cut and install shelves between the dividers. Construct and install drawers. (See page 86 for complete directions.)

If the dividers are to contain shelves that will rest on cleats, fasten the cleats to the dividers before you install them. If you're using shelf clips that will fit into predrilled holes, drill the holes before you install the dividers. If the dividers will contain drawers, attach the drawer supports at this point.

Mark locations for closet pole hangers and install them. (If you want several poles, you will need additional side cleats to hold the extra hangers.) Measure and cut the poles and drop them into place.

A second shelf 12 inches above the first shelf provides storage space for little-used items. If you want a second shelf, install it last.

Prefabricated modular units are usually assembled on-site. They may require no fasteners other than those supplied with the unit. Install these units according to the instructions included in the package.

A combination installation procedure may be desirable with nonwood closet units. For example, plastic-covered metal standards, shelves, and baskets have found widespread use in residential construction and are reasonably economical. When using these install the main shelf first. Next, install the upper storage shelf. Then purchase the unit of your choice to fill the space below the main shelf most efficiently. Modular units come in a wide variety of sizes and shapes; choose the ones that best fit your needs.

Multipurpose and Specific-Use Closets

Closets in family or activity rooms usually require more shelving than clothes closets and seldom have poles. Linen closets ordinarily contain a series of shelves, located at heights convenient to the user. Guest rooms usually have small traditional closets.

Closet Doors

Choose a conventional swinging door (see page 99 for how to trim) or a sliding (bypass) door or an accordion (bifold) door (see illustration).

Bypass doors come either ¾ inch or 1⅜ inches thick. They are mounted on an exposed upper track or on a track built into the head jamb.

For a built-in track, the doors and the frame are ordered as a unit. Cover the gap between the frame and the finished wall surface with casing.

A less expensive method is to frame the rough opening (either top and sides or across the top only) with 1-by jamb stock cut as wide as the wall is thick (including wallboard on both sides). Nail this frame to the header and the trimmers. Measure and cut a length of sliding-door track and screw it to the head jamb. Position the track to allow for the thickness of the doors (and a trim valance, if one is needed).

Trim the door panels to size, if necessary, and attach roller hardware to the top corners on the back of each door. Lift the doors onto the track (tilt them in order to do so), and check for fit and smooth operation. To make adjustments loosen the

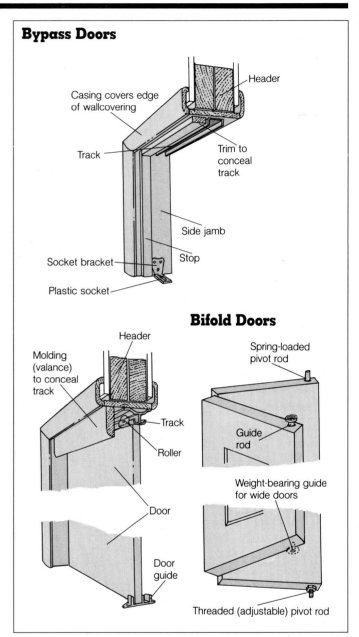

Bypass Doors

Casing covers edge of wallcovering

Header

Track

Trim to conceal track

Side jamb

Socket bracket

Stop

Plastic socket

Bifold Doors

Header

Molding (valance) to conceal track

Track

Roller

Door

Door guide

Spring-loaded pivot rod

Guide rod

Weight-bearing guide for wide doors

Threaded (adjustable) pivot rod

screws in the roller hardware and lower or raise the door as necessary. Tighten the screws before removing the doors in order to mount the valance.

Attach the valance either by screwing it directly to the finish wall or by hanging it from corner angles mounted to the head jamb. (Make sure that the doors will clear the valance.)

Apply casing around the opening. Rehang the doors and screw or nail stops and guides into the finish floor.

Installation of bifold doors is the same as that for bypass doors; only the hardware differs. If the door has two panels and is more than 3 feet wide, support the sliding end with a special weight-bearing slider. On narrower doors a simple locating pin is sufficient.

Contemporary Closet

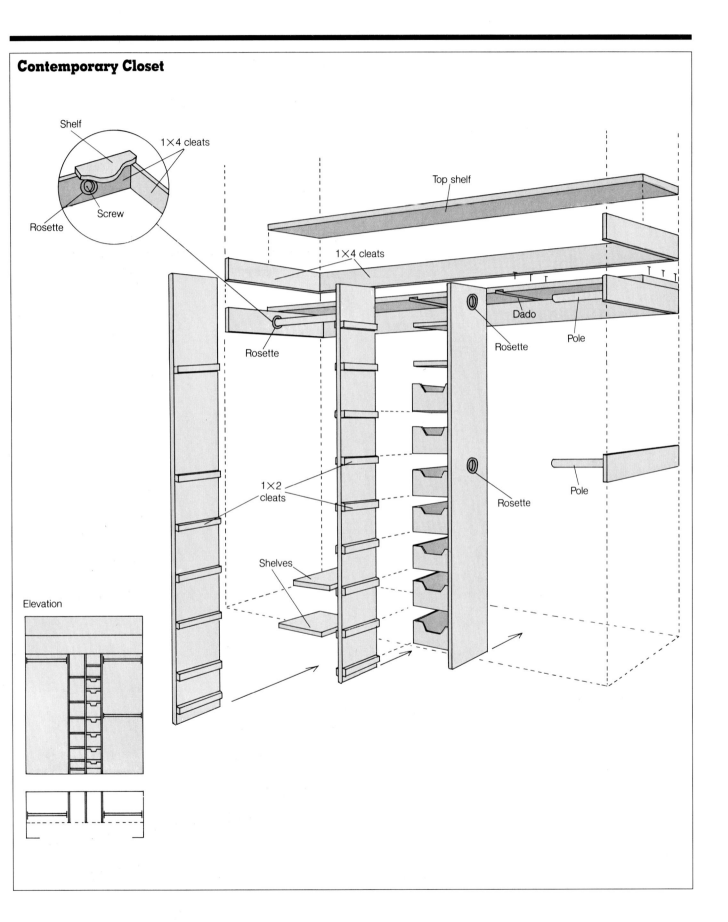

Shelf

1×4 cleats

Screw

Rosette

Top shelf

1×4 cleats

Rosette

Dado

Rosette

Pole

Pole

1×2 cleats

Shelves

Rosette

Elevation

CABINETS

Cabinets are the showpiece of most kitchens. They represent a large share of the cost of renovation as well. If you would like to extend your finish carpentry skills and make your own cabinets, the following explanations will guide you through the process.

Nowadays, however, it is standard practice to construct the units completely before installing them. This approach is quicker, easier, and much less awkward.

Since it is usually simpler to attach the wall cabinets before the base units are in place, make the former first. Remember that full cabinets are very heavy. Always use strong joints and always fasten each unit to the studs.

Standard manufactured wall cabinets are usually 12 inches

Organize the Sequence of Construction

Begin by grouping the construction into phases. The first phase is cutting and assembling the basic case: ends, partitions, fixed shelves, bottom, and back. The second phase is attaching the face frame. It can be completely assembled first and then attached to the base as a unit, or it can be glued and nailed to the base in separate pieces. The third phase is building the doors and drawers, and the fourth phase is making toe kicks and underlayments for the lower units.

To begin each phase, prepare a detailed cut list of all the pieces that you will need. A cut list is simply a list of cabinet parts in the final cut size. It is important to make a complete list for each phase in order not to waste stock. For instance, if you know ahead of time that you will need three 36-inch pieces of 1 by 2, you can use a 10-foot length instead of three 4-foot lengths.

Wall Cabinets

Until recently the traditional method of installing wall and base cabinets was to build and fasten them to the wall piece by piece.

Noticing some of the details in these solid cherry cabinets crafted by a fine cabinetmaker will help when planning your own kitchen. The colonial style of the room is enhanced by paneled lipped doors (see page 85) and exposed offset H-hinges painted flat black.

Wall Cabinet Construction

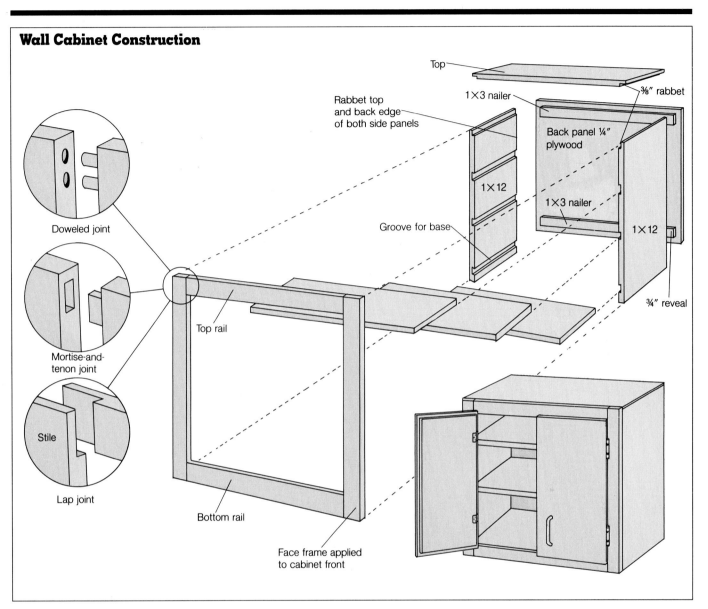

Doweled joint

Mortise-and-tenon joint

Stile

Lap joint

Top rail

Bottom rail

Face frame applied to cabinet front

Rabbet top and back edge of both side panels

Groove for base

Top

1×3 nailer

⅜" rabbet

Back panel ¼" plywood

1×12

1×3 nailer

1×12

¾" reveal

deep and are generally fastened to the wall 18 inches above the countertop. You can use any dimensions you like, but the standard dimensions provide the most efficient clearance.

Constructing Wall Cabinets

1. Using 1 by 12 appearance-grade stock, cut the side, top, and bottom pieces of the cabinet to length. If you prefer, cut these pieces out of plywood that is finished on both sides.

Cut rabbets in the side pieces to accept the top of the cabinet and the plywood back, and dadoes to accept the bottom of the cabinet and the shelves. (The depth of the dado cuts should be ⅜ inch.) If you prefer adjustable shelves, see page 92. The dado for the bottom of the cabinet should be positioned to allow the face frame to cover the edge (see illustration). Apply glue to the ends of the bottom

of the cabinet, fit the bottom into the dadoes of each side piece, and nail the bottom in place with 4d finishing nails. Fit the top of the cabinet into the rabbets on each side piece (after applying glue to the edges) and nail in place.

2. Set the cabinet on its face in order to install the back 1 by 3 nailing cleats. Square up the cabinet. Glue and fasten the ¼-inch plywood back in place, preferably with staples or cement-coated nails.

3. Set the cabinet on its back. Cut the shelves to length (remember to allow for the depth of the dadoes). Apply glue to the edge of the shelves at each end, slide the shelves into the cabinet, and nail them in place.

4. Cut 1 by 2 strips for the face frame and assemble it, using either doweled, mortise and tenon, or lap joints. (Correct measurements are essential, since the frame determines the dimensions of the door opening.) Glue and clamp the joints. Wipe off excess glue with a damp cloth before it sets. When it is dry nail the face frame to the front edges of the cabinet. Set all nails and fill the holes.

Base Cabinets

When you make your own cabinets, you can design them to suit yourself. However, remember that appliances such as dishwashers, stoves, ovens, and refrigerators are made to fit standard-sized cabinets. For kitchen base cabinets the standard dimensions are 35¼ inches high (not including the countertop) and 24 inches deep. Bathroom vanity cabinets are generally 30 inches high, although 36-inch cabinets are becoming more popular. The width of the vanity is determined by the size and shape of the washbasin.

If you have a long line of base cabinets, such as a kitchen peninsula or wall unit, you can either build it as a single assembly or build several smaller units and attach them together, as described for wall cabinets on page 87.

Constructing Base Cabinets

1. From ¾-inch stock cut two side panels 23¼ inches by 35¼ inches. Cut a 3½-inch-square notch at the lower front corner of each panel. See illustration.

2. On the inner side of each panel, dado a ¾-inch-wide by ⅜-inch-deep groove from front to back. The bottom edge of the groove should be even with the top of the 3½-inch notch. These

Base Cabinet Construction

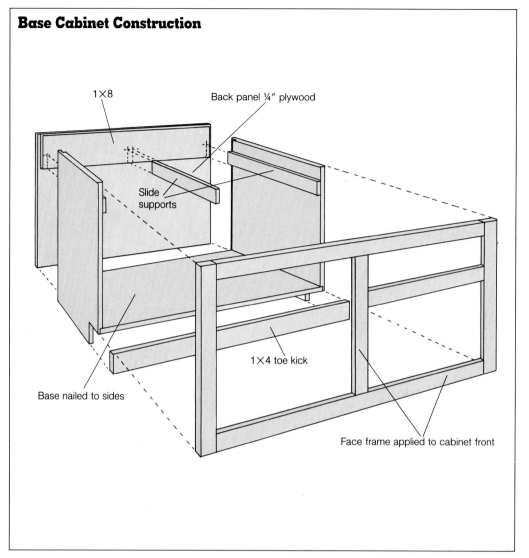

1×8

Back panel ¼" plywood

Slide supports

Base nailed to sides

1×4 toe kick

Face frame applied to cabinet front

grooves will support the bottom panel. Cut a ⅜-inch-wide by ¼-inch-deep rabbet on the inside back edge of each side piece. These rabbets will accept the back panel, which will be cut out of ¼-inch plywood. Dado additional grooves if you plan to install any fixed shelves or adjustable shelf standards (see page 92); or drill holes for adjustable shelf supports.

3. From ¾-inch sheet material cut a base panel 23 inches wide by the length of the cabinet less ¾ inch. From 1 by 8 stock cut a nailer the length of the cabinet less ½ inch.

4. Following the sequence described for the wall cabinets, assemble the pieces, using glue and nails. Check for square. Then hold in position while you nail the plywood back.

5. Make a face frame out of 1 by 2 clear stock. Cut two stiles (vertical pieces) to the full face length of the sides. Cut the rails

(horizontal pieces) to fit between them. Cut stiles for the vertical dividers (mullions) and rails for the drawer divisions. Glue, clamp, and assemble the frame before attaching it to the cabinet; wipe all excess glue from joints before glue dries. Mount the frame in place with finishing nails. Set all nails and fill the holes.

Cabinet Doors

Hinged doors can be flush-mounted, full-overlay, or lipped. See illustration to compare the styles and the hardware required for each.

Flush Doors

Cut doors to match the size of the opening; they will lie flush with the outside face of the frame. An inset European-style hinge is the most popular type. With this type of hinge, holes are bored on the inside of the door to accommodate the wafer section of the hinge so that it will fit snug and flush. The other section of the hinge mounts on the inside of the cabinet. Although it costs a good deal, this type of hinge is popular because you can make wide adjustments to align the doors. Butt or pivot hinges are a less expensive option.

Full-Overlay Doors

Cut the doors to match the outside dimensions of the face frame. The full-overlay European-style hinge is the most popular choice for this type of cabinet door. You can also use butt hinges screwed to the front face of the frame and the inside face of the door, or angled or flat pivot hinges screwed to the top and underside of the cabinet and the inside face of the door.

Lipped Doors

These are a combination of full-overlay and flush doors. The inside face fits inside the opening, and the outside face overlaps the frame. Cut the doors to a size that gives the desired

amount of overlap; then cut rabbets around the edges. If there is a divider in the cabinet, or if the cabinet has only one door, rabbet all four edges. If there are double doors but no divider, do not rabbet the edge that butts against the other door. Use semiconcealed ⅜-inch inset self-closing hinges

for mounting the doors. (The narrow leaf will be exposed on the face frame.)

Door Hardware

Most hinges nowadays are spring loaded and do not require any special type of catch. However, in cases where special catches are needed, there are many types to choose from.

Mount each catch beneath one of the shelves or on a mullion or stile, so that it will be out of the way. The choice of knobs, pulls, and handles is also a matter of personal preference. To mount, carefully mark all doors so that the knobs align horizontally and, if possible, vertically as well.

Cabinet Doors and Hinges

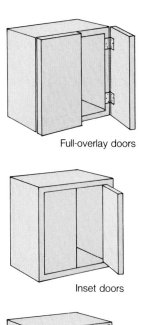

Full-overlay doors

Inset doors

Lipped doors

Butt hinge

Butt hinge

Semiconcealed hinge

Pivot hinge

Pivot hinge
(1 leaf
screwed to
top or bottom
of case)

European-style hinge

European-style hinge

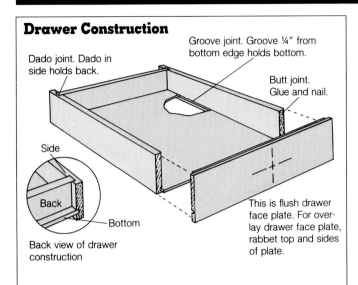

Drawer Construction

Dado joint. Dado in side holds back.

Groove joint. Groove ¼" from bottom edge holds bottom.

Butt joint. Glue and nail.

Side

Back

Bottom

Back view of drawer construction

This is flush drawer face plate. For overlay drawer face plate, rabbet top and sides of plate.

Drawers

A drawer is simply an open-faced box. It can be made out of ½-inch or ⅜-inch board stock, plywood, or special high-pressure particleboard. The latter material, which is coated with a tough, scratch-resistant laminate, is becoming very popular. Traditionally the sides of drawers were dovetailed into the front and back piece to make solid joints. If you don't own a dovetail jig for your router, use dadoes and grooves to make a strong drawer. See illustration.

1. Cut the side and front pieces to length and cut dado grooves in them to receive the base of the drawer. These grooves should be ¼ inch from the bottom of each piece. Cut the back piece to length and dado the side pieces to accept the back. Assemble the pieces; if they fit, glue and nail the sides together. Apply glue to the edges of the base, slide

it into the grooves on the side pieces, and clamp until dry.

2. For a full overlay drawer, the face plate should overlap the drawer opening by about ½ inch on all four sides. Cut the face plate to length out of ½-inch or ¾-inch appearance-grade stock. If you wish you can carve a design on the front or chamfer the edges with a router. Attach the face plate to the drawer with two screws. Use screws long enough to grip, but not to penetrate, the plate. Make sure that the face plate is centered on the opening rather than on the drawer. (The slides may make the drawer sit slightly off center.)

3. Drawers can be supported by slides mounted on each side of the drawer cavity. For side supports to hold the slides, nail 1 by 2 rails to the outer walls of the cabinet and 2 by 2 rails to the verticle center partition and to an additional vertical support placed between the cabinet floor and the rear wall support.

4. It is easier to install the sliding hardware before the countertop is in place, so do

this next. The local building-supply outlet should have a variety of mechanisms from which to choose. It is also easier to install the counter supports now. Nail them between the rear wall support and the face frame every 2 feet, except where you need a larger opening for the sink.

Installing Cabinets

Whether you have constructed your own kitchen cabinets or purchased ready-made units, installing them is a meticulous and demanding task. It's easy to underestimate the time required to do it right. For a kitchen of average size, figure on putting in about a week of work.

In a successful cabinet installation, the units are level, plumb, and square; all joints are tight and flush; and the doors and drawers are aligned. Carefully study the following techniques, and the manufacturer's instructions if you're installing purchased units, before you start to work. The following description applies to purchased units, but it can also be used for units that you've constructed yourself. Note especially the differences between frame and frameless cabinet installations. There is no margin for error with frameless cabinets; if they are not perfectly square and straight, then the doors and drawers will not fit properly.

Preparation

Cabinets are installed relatively late in the construction sequence. All the walls and ceilings should be smooth, and the soffits, if any, should be finished, unless you are adding them later. Painting should be completed, wallcoverings may be up, and wiring for under-counter lighting should be installed. If the finish floor is down, protect it with plywood or cardboard while the cabinets are being installed. Remove paintings and other valuable objects from the walls.

The tools you will need are a ⅜-inch or ¼-inch electric drill, preferably variable-speed; a countersink bit; an assortment of screwdrivers; a tape measure; a hammer; 2-foot and 4-foot levels; a 6-foot straightedge or a long level; adjustable clamps or C-clamps; a stepladder; shims; a flat prybar; masking tape; and a bar of soap. An extra electric drill with a Phillips-screwdriver bit is handy to have. You will also need a supply of 1½-inch, 2½-inch, and 3-inch quick-drive wood screws; 3d, 4d, and 6d finishing nails; 1-inch brads; and whatever special connecting screws are provided with frameless cabinets.

Inspect all the cabinets for defects and verify the sizes. Make sure that the doors fit, that none of the boxes is warped, and that all the drawers slide perfectly. Remove all the doors; mark on each door which cabinet it belongs with; and put the cabinets back into the cartons. Store them until you need them.

Start the layout for the cabinets by locating the highest point of the floor in the area where the base units will be installed. See illustration on page 88. Use a long level or a straightedge with a level on it. If the highest point is not against the wall, use a level and a pencil to transfer the height of that point to the wall. Having marked the wall at the appropriate height, measure up from the mark and make a second mark at the height of the base cabinets (usually 34½ inches). Add an allowance for the thickness of the finish floor if it is not yet down and make a third mark. Using the straightedge and a level, draw a line on the wall at this third mark. This line represents the tops of all the base cabinets. (The line will be covered by the counter or the backsplash. Make heavy marks on the wall only where they will be covered; elsewhere use a faint pencil line.)

Now draw another level line for the tops of the wall cabinets. Most wall cabinets are 30 inches tall and are positioned 18 inches above the countertop. For most installations, then, this line will be exactly 84 inches (36 + 18 + 30) above the highest point of the floor.

If the wall cabinets extend up to a soffit or up to the ceiling, check them for level. Find the lowest point of the ceiling or soffit in the area over the cabinets and draw a level line on the wall at that height for the cabinet tops. You can now see how much of a gap

there will be between the ceiling or soffit and the cabinets. After the cabinets are installed, cover this gap with a strip of molding.

If the installation includes a full-height cabinet, measure it now to make sure that it will fit beneath the ceiling or soffit. You may have to trim the top or the base, according to the manufacturer's instructions.

Using the lines on the wall for horizontal guides and a level for plumb, lay out the cabinet dimensions on the wall. Make sure that they line up properly with each other and with the various corners, windows, sinks, appliances, and so forth. Make any necessary adjustments.

Next, mark the location of each stud just above the line for the base cabinets, in the area where the upper cabinets will be hung. To find a stud, tap lightly on the wall and listen for a solid sound. Probe the area with a hammer and nail until you locate both edges of the stud. Mark the exact center of the stud on the wall. Using a level, draw a vertical line through this mark. Repeat for each stud behind the upper cabinets. If there is blocking between the studs, mark a horizontal line at the center of the blocking where the cabinets will be hung.

It is usually easier to install the wall cabinets before the base cabinets. However, if the back splash will be full-height laminate that extends up to the wall cabinets, the base cabinets and the countertop must be installed first. It is also better to install the base cabinets first if there is a full-height cabinet in the middle of a run.

Installing Wall Cabinets

Start a run of wall cabinets with a full-height unit or a corner unit if you have one. Otherwise start at whichever end will not require a filler piece. The first cabinet is the most critical—it must be perfectly level, plumb, and square, or the entire run will be out of alignment.

Measure where the studs line up behind the first cabinet and transfer these measurements to the inside of the cabinet at the top and bottom hanger rails. See illustration on page 88. Countersink and drill holes through the back of the cabinet at these marks; make the holes just large enough for the 3-inch screws.

If the cabinets are frameless, they may require a metal support rail, provided by the manufacturer. Install this rail next. It must be attached to the wall behind the cabinets, which will be hung from it. Cut the rail to length and screw it securely to each stud at the height recommended by the manufacturer.

There are several methods for holding the cabinets in place while you attach them to the wall. One is to build a T-brace slightly longer than the distance between the floor and the bottom of the cabinet. Another method, used when the base cabinets are installed first, is to build a simple rectangular frame out of 2 by 4s; this frame should be just high enough to support the wall cabinets when it sits on a makeshift countertop. A third method can be

used if the walls have not yet been finished. Simply screw a 1-by cleat to the wall to support the bottom of the cabinets. A specialty jack is useful here, if you know a professional who might lend you one.

To begin, lift the first cabinet into place and slide the brace up under it. You will need a helper to stabilize the cabinet while you do this. Attach the cabinet to the studs with 3-inch screws, tightening only one of the top screws and leaving the others slightly loose. Place a shim behind the cabinet, next to a screw, at any point where the wall bows inward. Use a level to check that the cabinet is plumb and horizontal in all directions.

Now transfer the stud dimensions to the inside of the second cabinet and countersink and drill the screw holes. Drill two more screw holes through the vertical stile on the side that will be attached to the first cabinet. Drill where the hinges will cover up the screw heads.

For frameless cabinets the side holes are already partially drilled, about 3 inches back and 2 to 3 inches up from the bottom or down from the top. Simply complete the drilling. Special fasteners go into these holes; they screw into each other, leaving a smooth head on each side that is covered with a plastic cap.

Lift the second cabinet into place and support it, but do not screw it into the back wall. Instead, clamp the two cabinets together so that the joint between them is tight and flush. Use wood shims to protect the cabinet finish from the clamps. Choose a drill bit slightly smaller than the shank of a 1½-inch screw and center it in the

Cabinet Layout

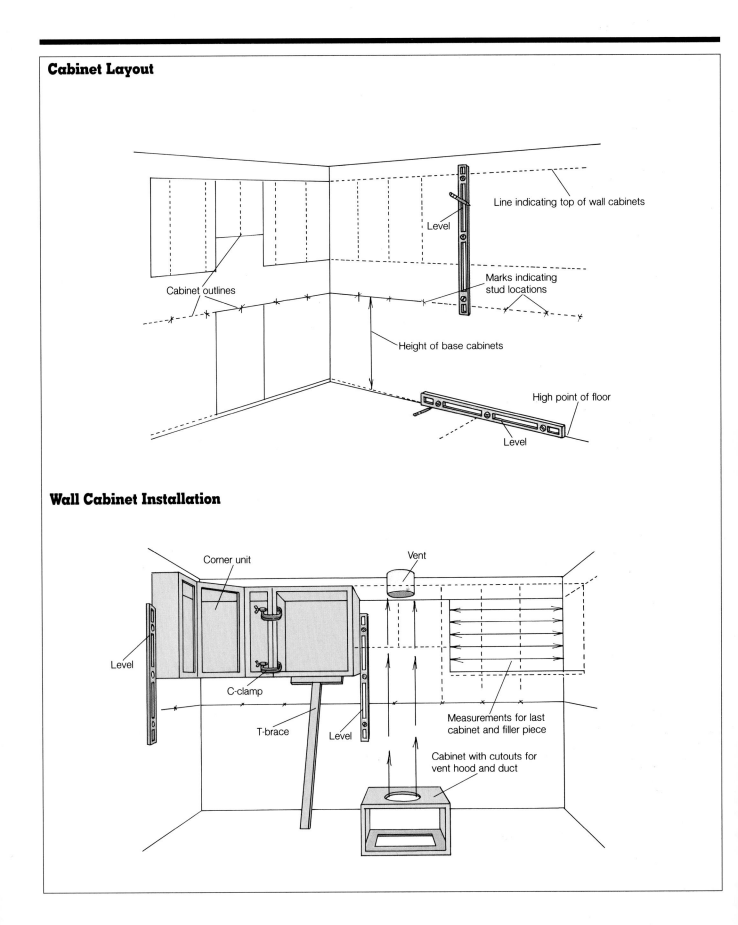

Line indicating top of wall cabinets

Level

Cabinet outlines

Marks indicating stud locations

Height of base cabinets

High point of floor

Level

Wall Cabinet Installation

Corner unit

Vent

Level

C-clamp

T-brace

Level

Measurements for last cabinet and filler piece

Cabinet with cutouts for vent hood and duct

Base Cabinet Installation

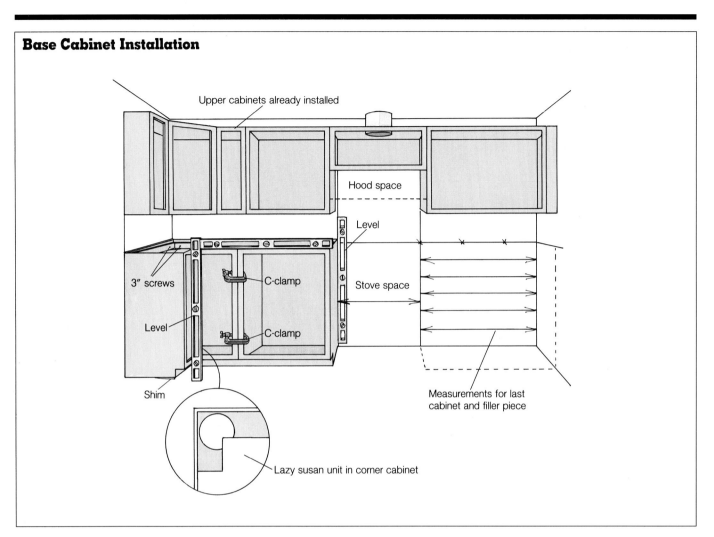

Upper cabinets already installed

Hood space

Level

Stove space

3" screws

C-clamp

Level

C-clamp

Shim

Measurements for last
cabinet and filler piece

Lazy susan unit in corner cabinet

first side hole of the second cabinet. Drill about two thirds of the way into the adjoining stile of the first cabinet.

Do the same for the second side hole. Now lubricate two 1½-inch screws with bar soap and drive them firmly into the holes that you have just drilled. If the cabinets are tall or if the face frames do not align perfectly, predrill more holes and add more screws. Then attach the cabinet to the back wall, in the same way as you did the first cabinet.

Repeat this process for all the wall cabinets in the same

run. If a vent hood will be mounted to a wall cabinet, cut holes in the cabinet for the duct before you install the cabinet.

If the final cabinet will end next to a sidewall, there may be a gap that needs a filler piece. These come in 3-inch and 6-inch widths and must be cut to fit snugly. Before you install that cabinet, attach the filler piece to the stile in the same way as you would attach two cabinets together. Then take a series of measurements between the wall and the last

cabinet installed. Transfer these measurements to the face of the final cabinet, marking them on the filler piece. Now connect the marks with a line. Cut along the line with a fine-toothed keyhole saw, angling the back of the cut toward the cabinet. The cut will follow any deviations in the wall so that the filler piece will fit perfectly. Filler pieces for corners are installed in the same way, but they need not be scribed and cut. Some manufacturers provide cabinets with wide stiles, called ears, already attached. These ears function as filler

pieces and are trimmed in the same way.

When the full run of wall cabinets is in place, check for level, plumb, and square (measure diagonals). Use shims to make any necessary adjustments, loosening the back screws to slip the shims into place. After all the screws are tightened, make a final check. Be especially careful with frameless cabinets. The slightest warp will make the doors hang crooked.

Installing Base Cabinets

Frame and frameless base units are installed in the same way as wall cabinets, except that with the frameless style there is no margin for error. Start with a corner unit, unless a cabinet in the middle of a run must be perfectly aligned with some other feature, such as a window or the sink plumbing. Set the cabinet in place and shim under the base until the top is even with the layout line. Countersink and drill through the top rail at each stud and attach the rail to the stud with 3-inch screws. If the wall is not straight, place shims behind the cabinet, using a level to check the top, sides, and front. Hold the level against the frame and not against a door or drawer.

Set the second unit in place and attach it to the first unit, using the method described on page 87 for wall cabinets. Screw it to the back wall. See illustration on page 89.

Complete the run of base cabinets. Some of them, such as lazy susan corner units and sink fronts, have no box to attach to the wall. They are held in place only at the face frames. (With frameless styles the sink fronts have sides that extend back just far enough to attach them to the adjacent cabinets.) Because these units have no backs, you will have to provide support for the countertop along the backside. Screw cleats of 1-by lumber to the wall just below the layout line.

You will also need to fabricate a floor for some sink fronts. Cut it out of a piece of ½-inch to ¾-inch plywood and support it on cleats screwed to the wall and to the adjacent cabinets. Seal it or paint it before you install it.

If there will be an appliance in the middle of a run—a dishwasher, trash compactor, or slide-in range—you must allow for it when you install the base cabinets. Check the appliance specifications to determine the exact width of the space. To keep the cabinets on both sides aligned, bridge the gap with a long straightedge at the front and back. Install filler pieces at the end of the run and at the corners, just as you did for the wall cabinets.

Finishing Touches

Finish panels, doors, trim, and handles are the most noticeable features of a cabinet installation. Take care to attach them correctly. Try to set aside one day just to do this part of the job; don't try to do it at the end of a long day's work.

In some lines of manufactured cabinets, finish panels must be installed on all the exposed faces of every unit. These panels come either precut or as a full sheet of plywood paneling from which you cut out each piece to fit. If the panels have grain patterns, match each one carefully with the patterns on the adjacent cabinets.

Measure and cut each panel to size. Spread contact cement on the back of each panel and

Cabinet Finishes

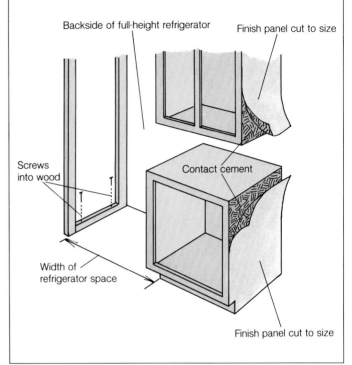

on the side of the cabinet where the panel will be positioned. Let it set for the amount of time given in the instructions. Press the panel in place, clamp it, and leave it overnight to dry. See illustration. If necessary, use 3d nails to help hold it in place. The nail heads can be countersunk and the holes filled with putty after the cement dries.

When you put the doors back on the cabinets, some of them may not line up perfectly. Most hinges have a mechanism for making slight adjustments to correct this problem.

Before you install trim pieces, be sure that the cabinets are aligned and securely fastened. Cut the trim to length with a miter box, and stain or paint the trim, including the cut ends, before you attach it. Predrill the trim and fasten it with 3d, 4d, or 6d finishing nails. Sink the heads with a nail set and fill the holes.

For frameless units attach the trim pieces from inside the cabinet, using screws. Predrill holes through the cabinet large enough to take the screws; use a smaller bit to drill pilot holes in the trim itself. Most manufacturers provide plastic caps to cover the screw heads.

To finish the toe kick, cut baseboard or similar molding to length and paint or stain it a dark color. Attach it to the cabinet kicks with finishing nails.

HELVES

You can use shelves in almost every room of the house: for cookware in the kitchen, for towels in the bathroom, for books in the den, for china in the dining room. Shelves are also necessary in kitchen and bathroom cabinets and in linen and miscellaneous storage closets.

Types of Shelves

There are two distinct types of shelves. One is custom-fitted between two sidewalls and a rear wall in a closet. The other is square cut and positioned between two finished side pieces in a cabinet or bookcase. The first is permanently fastened in place; the second can be either permanently fastened or adjustable.

Fitted Shelves

Custom-fitted shelves are used in closets and freestanding bookcases.

In Closets

To make custom-fitted shelves for a closet, start by measuring between the sidewalls at the height for each shelf. For closets with several shelves, start at the bottom and work your way up. (The cleats should be in place; see page 79.) Take measurements between the sidewalls at the front and the back of the closet; they will probably not be parallel to each other or square with the rear wall. Walls are seldom exactly true.

Now check the corners with a framing square. Position the long leg of the square against the rear wall and move it toward a corner. If the corner of the framing square touches the sidewall before the short leg touches it, note the gap between the wall and the short leg of the square. Repeat this procedure at the opposite sidewall. If there is a gap on both

Fitting a Closet Shelf

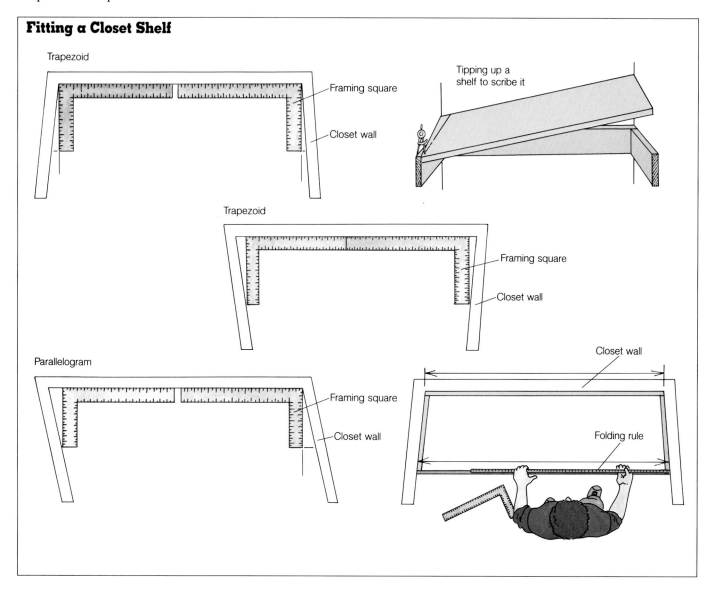

Trapezoid — Framing square — Closet wall

Tipping up a shelf to scribe it

Trapezoid — Framing square — Closet wall

Parallelogram — Framing square — Closet wall

Closet wall — Folding rule

sides, the shelf board will be trapezoidal when it is cut to fit. If the short leg of the framing square touches the sidewall before the corner of the square meets the corner of the wall, and if this happens on both sides, the shelf board will once again be trapezoidal. If the corners touch first at one side and the short leg touches first at the other, the shelf board will be shaped like a parallelogram (see illustration on page 91).

If the space is a trapezoid or a parallelogram, add 1 inch to the longest dimension of your measurement to allow for scribing and making final cuts on the board. Cut the board to this length. Position it in place, tipped up at one end, and mark the other end with a scriber set at the width of the gap. Saw along this line, starting with a square cut at the front of the board and back-cutting as you progress. Hold this cut against the wall to test it. Correct it with a rasp if necessary.

Transfer the longest measurement between the sidewalls to the board. Position it in place, tipped the opposite way. Set the scriber to this mark and scribe the board. Saw the board as described above and place it in position. If the fit is a little tight, correct it with the rasp. With the shelf in place, scribe it and fit it to the rear wall.

In Bookcases

The shelves in a freestanding bookcase fit into dadoes in the uprights, just like the shelves for cabinets. The only difference is that bookcases have no back frame. If you want a bookcase backing, a thin sheet of plywood or hardboard adds stability and gives a finished look.

Adjustable Shelves

These can be mounted in one of several different ways. See illustration.

Holes and Dowels

Mark and drill parallel rows of holes down each side of the cabinet or bookcase. Do this carefully so that the shelves will lie flat and level. Drill the holes $\frac{3}{16}$ inch in diameter and $\frac{1}{2}$ inch deep, and space them at 2-inch intervals to provide flexibility in arranging the shelves. Cut lengths of $\frac{3}{16}$-inch dowel into 1-inch pieces. Use these pieces as shelf supports.

Holes and Clips

Drill the holes as described above, but instead of dowel, plug them with metal clips available at most hardware stores and building-supply outlets. Drill test holes on a scrap of wood to determine which bit gives the best fit.

Standards and Clips

Inexpensive metal shelf standards are readily available. They can be screwed directly onto alcove walls (over studs) or dadoed into the sides of a bookcase or cabinet. Special clips snap into the slots.

Standards and Brackets

Shelf brackets lock into standards that are screwed onto the back wall of an alcove over the studs or onto the sides of a bookcase. Choose brackets long enough for the hook on the end to slip over the front edge of the shelf, or cut a slot in the underside of the shelf to accept the hook.

Shelf Supports

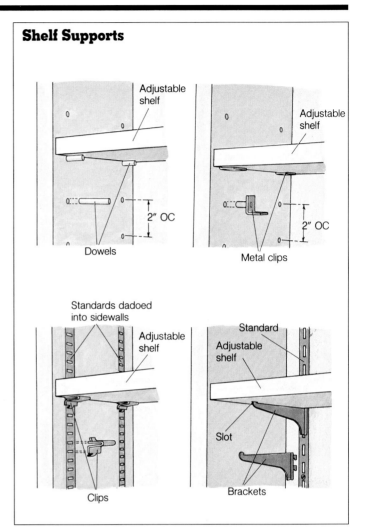

Dowels

Metal clips

Standards dadoed into sidewalls

Clips

Standard

Brackets

Installing Shelving

Most lines of ready-made cabinets include matching open-shelf units. You can also construct shelving of your own design from hardwood, plywood, or particleboard with a laminate covering. You can make a single shelf from an extra filler piece.

Adjustable shelves are recommended for large units. The simplest and least obtrusive way to build them is to drill a series of holes in the side of the unit into which small brackets can be inserted. These brackets will support the shelves.

There are several ways to harmonize the shelving with the cabinets. You can use the same kind of wood as was used for the cabinets and stain it or paint it to match. Use touch-up stain provided by the cabinet manufacturer. You may want to experiment first with scraps of the same wood. You can also harmonize the shelving with the cabinets by using the same moldings and trim. Finally, you can make the shelf unit the same height as the top of the wall cabinets and set the shelves at the same heights as the countertop, vent hood, and other prominent features.

INTERIOR STAIRS AND RAILINGS

The basic elements of stair building are the same indoors as out. Laying out and cutting the stringers is done in the same way; the differences are primarily in the finished appearance.

Compared to Exterior Installations

Exterior stairways are usually open and the materials used are weather resistant. Interior stairways take on a more finished look. This is mostly because they are generally, though not always, enclosed. Materials used are usually of higher quality than those used for exterior stairways, and a higher degree of finish is required. In addition, enclosed stairways usually have risers. When carpeting is to be installed as finish flooring, 1⅛-inch plywood is often used for the risers and treads.

Some applications of exterior enclosed stairways are similar to interior installations. Where code requirements dictate weathertight construction for exterior stairways, risers are necessary. In this case, the finished stairway will closely resemble an interior installation, although, of course, it will be more weatherproof. The design of the railings will usually differ, however.

Interior Details

If you were wise you laid temporary treads on the stair stringers during the heavy construction. Now that the messy part is over, you can install the finish treads, risers, posts, handrail, balusters, and trim. For detailed instructions on installing stairs, see the section starting on page 58.

Posts

Remove the temporary treads. Cut a hole in the subfloor large enough to allow you to attach the newel post firmly to the floor joists. (It may be necessary to notch the post or add blocking.) Use glue and carriage bolts or lag screws. Secure the post at the top of the stairs in the same way. See illustration on page 94.

Treads and Risers

Install the finish treads and the risers, taking care to fit them snugly around the posts. Commonly, risers are mitered where they join the finished stringer.

On housed stringers butt the treads and risers tightly against the wall. On open stringers overlap the treads but not the risers. Drive in glue-coated wedges of scrap wood underneath to hold the treads and risers in position.

Softwood tread stock commonly comes with a bullnose. If hardwood tread stock is used, a nose strip must be applied to the edge of the tread using glue and finish nails.

Handrail

There are several different ways to attach a handrail. You can use doweled butt joints,

On an enclosed staircase, which has no balustrade on either side, the handrail is attached directly to the wall with brackets made especially for this purpose.

Methods for Attaching Handrail to Newel Post

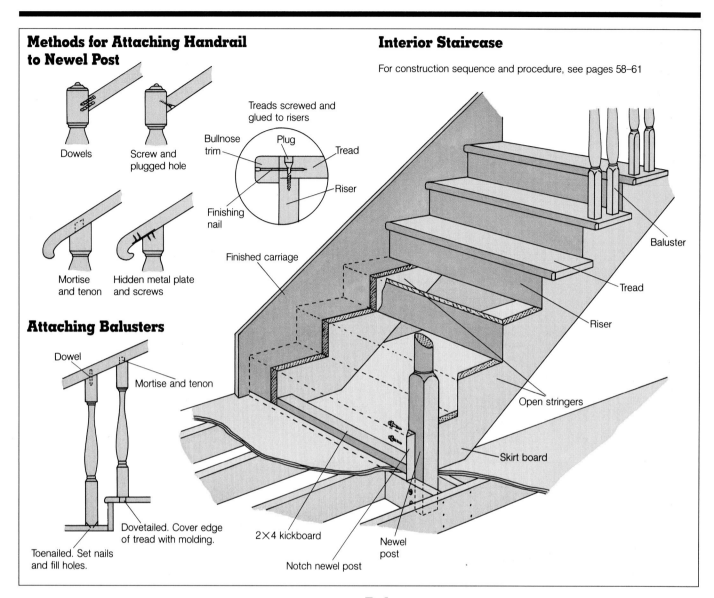

Dowels

Screw and plugged hole

Mortise and tenon

Hidden metal plate and screws

Treads screwed and glued to risers

Bullnose trim

Plug

Tread

Riser

Finishing nail

Attaching Balusters

Dowel

Mortise and tenon

Dovetailed. Cover edge of tread with molding.

Toenailed. Set nails and fill holes.

2×4 kickboard

Notch newel post

Interior Staircase

For construction sequence and procedure, see pages 58–61

Finished carriage

Baluster

Tread

Riser

Open stringers

Skirt board

Newel post

---

mortise-and-tenon joints, countersunk and plugged screws or bolts, or metal straps. The last method entails cutting a mortise on the underside of the handrail.

Position the handrail, but before you secure it, mark the position of each baluster. (Usually you will need two balusters per tread to meet code requirements.) Mark the position of the balusters on the treads. Then drop a plumb line

from the handrail. Carefully mark the position and angle of the plumb line on the rail.

If all or part of the staircase is enclosed and there is no balustrade on either side, you will have to attach a handrail to the wall. Building-supply outlets have brackets made especially for this purpose. Screw them to studs and attach the rail.

Balusters

These can be attached to the handrail either with a mortise-and-tenon joint or with dowels. To make sure that the balusters will be equidistant and plumb, drill the holes for the dowels or chisel the mortises at the marked points and at the correct angle.

Traditionally balusters were dovetailed into the treads, and molding was used to cover the dovetailing. An easier method is to drill pilot holes at an angle and screw or toenail the

balusters to the treads. When you have done this, position and attach the handrail.

Trim

Used creatively molding and quarter round can act as decorative accents while they conceal the joints. Use pieces of trim to cap a housed stringer and to finish off risers on an open one.

INTERIOR WINDOW TRIM

Your choice of interior casing will probably be dictated by design considerations. It may also be dictated by the need to match other trim in the house.

Compared to Exterior Installations

Interior installations are both similar to and different from exterior installations. Both cover the gap between the window jambs and the wallcovering and both are cut and fitted in essentially the same way. Differences occur primarily with picture frame casing, which requires the use of mitered cuts.

Correcting Flaws

Your first task, as with any finish work, is to check for flaws and to correct them. Look for jambs that protrude beyond the plane of the wallcovering. These make it nearly impossible to get good joints. Look too for jambs that don't quite meet the surface of the finish wall. In the former case, planing the jamb will usually solve the problem. See illustration. In the latter case, it may be necessary to install jamb extensions to bring the surfaces even, or to plane the wallboard. Finally, look for jambs that are bowed or curved. This flaw is usually corrected by straightening the jamb as the trim is nailed.

If the window frames are out of square, it's too late to correct them. You will have to make the necessary adjustments when you install the trim, by making cuts that match the angle of the frame. These cuts, then, will not necessarily be true 90-degree, or 45-degree, angles.

Window Trim Styles

Windows may be cased out in either of two styles. A picture frame installation consists of four identical casings, each mitered at a 45-degree angle. A stool-and-apron casing with a butted head exists in several variations. Sometimes, in fact, the head is not butted at all but mitered. See illustration on page 96. Before cutting any casing check the window frame for square by taking diagonals. A small discrepancy can usually be made up by adjusting the casing. If the window is substantially out of square, use a sliding bevel to determine the angle at each corner; transfer the angle to the mating casing piece and make the cut. Each corner will have a different angle, so you must check all of them.

Finally, remember to use finishing nails appropriate to the thickness of the casing. For example, for the most common casing—pine beveled—which is between 1⅝ inches and 2¼ inches wide and is ⅜ inch thick at the jamb side and ⅝ inch thick at the trimmer side, use 3d finishing nails at the jamb side and 6d finishing nails at the trimmer side. For the more traditional straight casing (usually Douglas fir), which is 3½ inches wide and ¾ inch thick, use 6d finishing nails at the jamb side and 8d finishing nails at the trimmer side.

Picture Frame Casing

This style of casing requires 45-degree mitered cuts. Although a handsaw and a miter box will get the job done, you can make these cuts faster and more smoothly with a power miter saw. Either way, the process is the same. It's the attention to detail that counts.

You may wish to practice on scrap material before you get started. When you're ready, lay

---

Planing Window Jamb and Wallboard

Planing window jamb

Planing wallboard

out the jambs for a constant reveal (normally 3/16 inch) all around the window (see illustration). Use a reveal gauge or a combination square and a sharp pencil or a knife blade. Starting with the head casing, cut a 45-degree miter on one end of a piece of trim and place the piece in its final position against the window frame. The short dimension of the miter should be at the reveal mark on the side jamb. Hold the piece firmly in place and mark the opposite end at the side jamb reveal mark. Cut a 45-degree miter at this end. Nail the casing to the jamb, starting at the center and working toward each end. Use appropriate-sized finishing nails spaced at 8 to 12 inches. Now nail the casing to the trimmer (through the wallcovering) at the same intervals. Be careful when you nail near the ends of a piece of casing; the wood may split. To avoid this, predrill a pilot hole or blunt the point of the nail before you drive it.

Next, cut 45-degree miters at each end of each side casing. Place the first piece in position against the miter of the head casing and check the fit. If it is satisfactory, carefully nail the side casing close to the miter, fastening it firmly in position. Nail down the wall, attaching the casing to the trimmer. If the window jamb is straight, nail

Determining Head Casing Length

Head casing length equals distance between side casings

Marking the Reveal

A combination square is used to mark reveal

Mark along top of blade, then turn combination square 90° and mark side jamb

3/16"

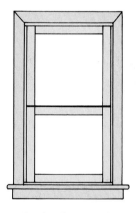

Window Trim Styles

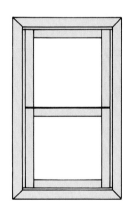

Mitered picture frame casing

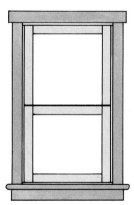

Stool and apron with butted head casing

Stool and apron with mitered head casing

Windowsill Construction

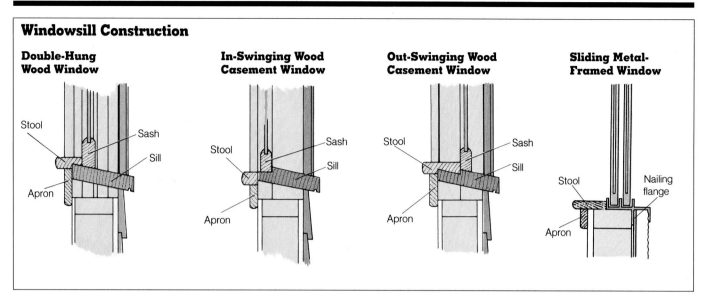

Double-Hung Wood Window

Stool — Sash — Sill — Apron

In-Swinging Wood Casement Window

Stool — Sash — Sill — Apron

Out-Swinging Wood Casement Window

Stool — Sash — Sill — Apron

Sliding Metal-Framed Window

Stool — Nailing flange — Apron

the casing to the jamb. If the jamb is curved, pull or push the casing into position as you nail. Repeat the procedure for the other side casing.

To install the bottom casing, cut a 45-degree miter at one end of a piece of material, place the cut against a side piece miter, and check the fit. Make adjustments if necessary. Reposition the piece and mark the opposite end at the place where it intersects with the other side casing. Now double-check the cut you are about to make. If the preceding miters are perfect (or very nearly so), a 45-degree cut on the bottom casing should fit exactly. However, even slight variations for which you have adjusted may cause a discrepancy in the final miter, so test the angle. Hold

the bottom casing in position for marking (tack it temporarily if you like). Mark the outside intersection point of the two casings. Then mark the inside intersection point. Make your cut between these two marks. If it is not a 45-degree angle, you can recut it by placing a wedge between the fence of the saw table or miter box and the casing to produce a slightly different angle. When using a power miter saw, it is possible to make cuts that are extremely close to the final cut, check the angle, and move the piece in the saw to make any adjustment, if necessary.

Place the adjusted casing in position, check for fit at the miter, and readjust as necessary. Nail the casing to the jamb in the center and in both directions. Finally, nail the casing to the trimmer.

Note: Since the bottom ends of the side casings are tacked in position, slight adjustments can usually be made at these miters by shifting the pieces as necessary to achieve a good fit.

When all the casings are installed, set all the nails and fill the nail holes.

Stool-and-Apron Casing With Butted Head

Trimming a window with a stool and apron is more complicated than trimming a picture frame window, even though there are few, if any, miter joints. If the head and side casings have the same dimensions, they can be mitered at the top. If they have different dimensions, they must be butted.

Stool

To trim a window with this style of casing, start with the stool. Stool stock is available in a variety of profiles; choose one that matches the windowsill. See illustration. The most common stools assume a sloped windowsill. For flat windowsills the stool can be 1-by material (the front edge can be rounded) that is cut to fit and simply butted against the sill or the window frame.

Begin by cutting the stool to the finished length. This length is equal to the inside distance between the jambs plus the lengths of the two horns. Each horn is equal to the width of the side casing, plus the reveal, plus the amount the stool extends beyond the side casing. See illustration on page 98.

Next, mark the centerlines of the sill and stool and hold the stool against the window opening, as shown in the illustration on page 98. If the window sash (or finished sill) is not parallel to the edge of the stool, scribe a cutting line along the stool with a compass. Cut along this line. Then, holding the stool with the centerlines aligned, position a combination square on the stool and push its blade tight to the finished jamb. Draw a light pencil line across the stool.

Determine the depth of each horn by setting a compass to the distance between the windowsill or window sash and the edge of the stool. Use this setting to scribe the stool parallel to the wall at the horns. This is the cut line; it ends at the

Marking and Cutting the Stool

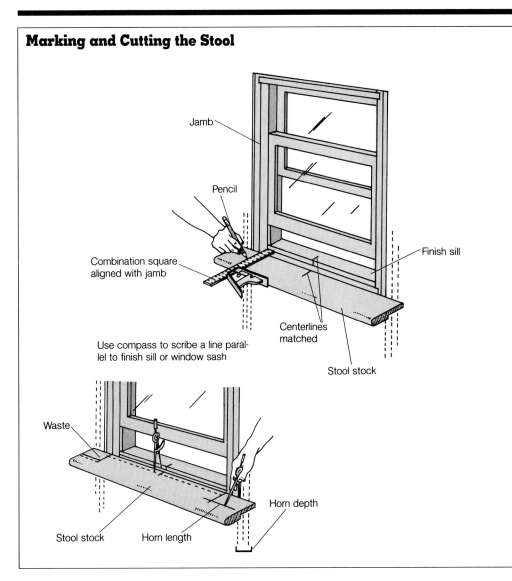

Jamb

Pencil

Combination square aligned with jamb

Use compass to scribe a line parallel to finish sill or window sash

Finish sill

Centerlines matched

Stool stock

Waste

Stool stock

Horn length

Horn depth

---

point where it intersects with the cut line of the jamb (the line scribed against the combination square).

Make these cuts with a jigsaw or a handsaw. If the jambs are not square, leave a little extra material at the horns as you cut; then plane or rasp it to fit. Place the stool in position and check to see that it is level and square. If necessary, insert shims under the stool to bring it up to the proper level relative to the windowsill or sash. (The stool should be about 3/16 inch

higher than the windowsill or the sash.) Use the appropriate-sized finishing nails to fasten the stool, driving them through the shims at 8 to 10 inches on center. On long horns nail horizontally through the horn into the trimmer.

Side Casings

Make the first casing by cutting a piece of stock square at one end and a little longer than the final length. Position the

squared end on the stool, aligning the edge of the piece with the reveal marks. If it doesn't fit, plane or rasp as necessary. When the fit is satisfactory, mark a cut line on the piece at the head casing reveal mark. Make a square cut at this line, position the piece, and tack it to the jamb and trimmer. Repeat for the other side casing.

If the side casings are to be mitered at the top, proceed as described above but at the reveal mark cut a 45-degree miter instead of a square cut. Then tack the casing in place.

Head Casing

Mark this casing by measuring the distance between the outside edges of the side casings and adding twice the amount of the head casing overhang. This dimension should equal the length of the stool. Position the head casing on top of the side casings and equalize the overhangs. If the butt joints are not tight, remove the side casings and adjust as necessary for fit and reveal. Fasten the casings to the trimmer and to the jamb with appropriate-sized finishing nails, spaced at about 12 inches on center.

A mitered head casing is installed like a picture frame casing (see page 95).

Apron

The material that you used for the side casings, or something similar, can be used for the apron, but the apron should not be wider than the casings, for aesthetic reasons. Measure the side casings, outside to outside, and cut the apron to that length. If the exposed end grain is unsuitable, it can be shaped with a router or a coping saw, or you can mount a return on the end of the apron to give it a finished appearance. Position the apron and drive the appropriate-sized finishing nails into the rough sill at about 12 inches on center. Then prop a temporary support under the apron and attach it by driving 6d finishing nails down through the stool into the top of the apron.

Door trim, or casing, is very similar to window trim: It can be mitered, butted, or butted with ornamental features added. The primary difference is that on a door there is no stool, apron, bottom casing, or sill. There may or may not be a threshold, depending on the floor covering. The joinery is the same, but the installation sequence may be different.

Mitered Casing

The two top joints of a mitered door casing are cut like those of a picture frame window casing. Only the bottom joints differ. See illustration.

Head Casing

Start by marking the reveals (which normally measure 3/16 inch) on the head and side jambs. Cut the head casing to length with miters on both ends and tack it in place precisely on these marks. Use appropriate-sized finishing nails to fasten the casing to the jamb and to the trimmer.

Side Casings

Measure the side casing dimension from the subfloor to the intersection of the head casing reveal mark and the side casing reveal mark. Miter one end of the casing and square-cut the other end. Hold the piece in position to the reveal marks and check the miter for fit. Adjust as necessary. If the finish floor is to be of wood, use a piece of this wood to scribe the bottom of the casing and cut at the mark. This will allow the casing to clear the finish floor. For carpeting allow ¼ inch of clearance from the subfloor. Repeat on the other side casing.

Butted Casing

A butt joint replaces a 45-degree miter in this type of door casing.

Head Casing

Center the head casing on top of the side casings, cut it to length, and nail it in place. If it doesn't fit flat, remove the side casings and trim the top of each one until you get a good fit. Reposition them, nail them securely, reposition the head casing, and nail.

Side Casings

Mark the reveal on all jambs. Begin by cutting a side casing slightly long and holding it in place, aligned with the reveal marks. If the casing does not fit flat on the floor, scribe and refit. If the finish floor will be of wood, slip a piece of this wood under the bottom of the casing and scribe to it. For carpeting allow about ¼ inch of clearance from the bottom of the casing to the subfloor. Hold one side casing and mark the point where the head casing reveal line intersects with the edge of the side casing. Cut and tack the side casing in position. Repeat for the other side casing.

Ornamental Butted Casing

When corner and plinth blocks are used, the plinth blocks are installed first. The side casings are installed next, then the corner blocks and the head casing.

Door Trim Styles

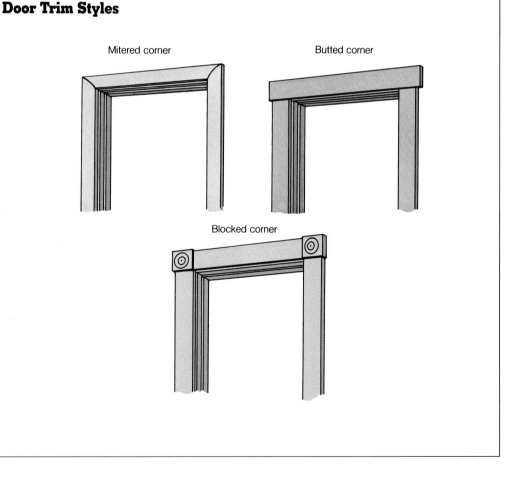

Mitered corner

Butted corner

Blocked corner

THER INTERIOR TRIM

Although improvements in materials and advances in construction methods have made it possible to create uniform, close-fitting surfaces, many people regard moldings as a necessary part of the decoration and apply them even when there are no gaps to cover.

Types of Trim

The most common types of trim are baseboard, which covers the joint where the walls meet the floor; ceiling trim, to cover the joint between the walls and the ceiling; picture rail, applied about a foot down from the top of a wall; and chair rail, attached to the wall about three feet from the floor to separate different wall treatments. See illustration. See pages 108 and 109 for suggestions on how to use standard trim for decorative effects.

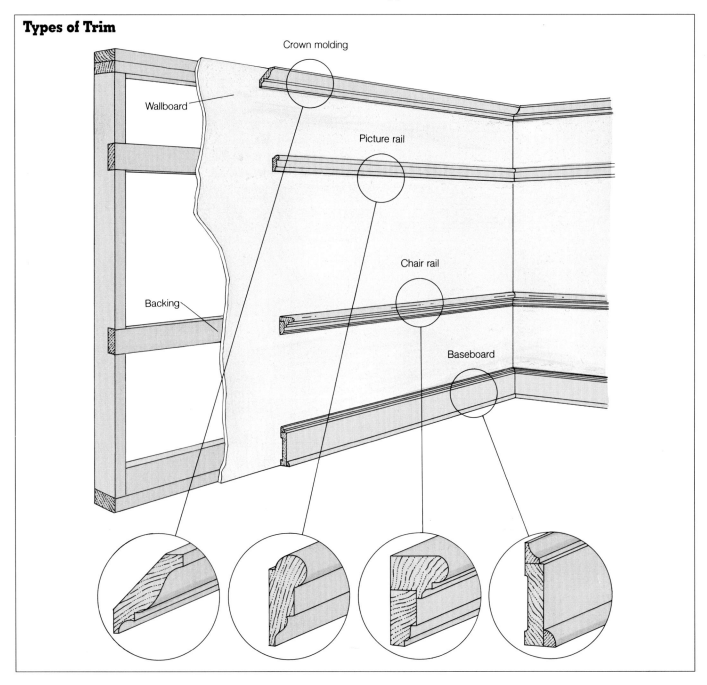

Types of Trim

Crown molding

Wallboard

Picture rail

Backing

Chair rail

Baseboard

Ceiling Trim

Flat Ceiling Trim With Wood Paneling

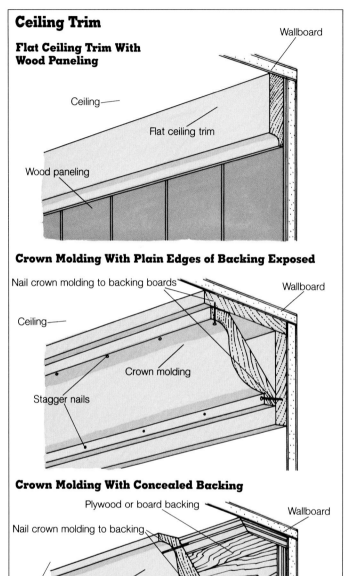

Crown Molding With Plain Edges of Backing Exposed

Crown Molding With Concealed Backing

Crown Molding Mitered at Outside Corner

Ceiling Trim Sequence

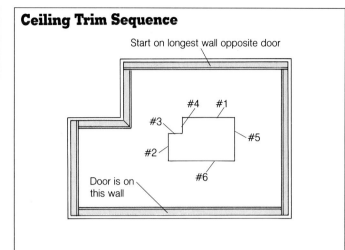

Working With Trim

Softwoods are commonly used for trim; hardwood trim is available, but it is more expensive. Because the milled shapes of trim strips are susceptible to damage, exercise great care when working with them. Trim should not be exposed to dampness—especially when it is unprimed. Milling puts a very smooth surface on the wood, and moisture will raise the grain; it will also cause the strips to bend, warp, and twist.

If you are recreating a traditional architectural style, or if you want to create a specific look, you can make your own trim. Refer to the discussion of shaping on page 33.

Installing Trim

Once you have completed the casing around the doors and windows, start installing the other trim. Work your way down from the top, starting with the ceiling trim and ending with the baseboard. There is nothing to stop you from using more than one strip if you are after a more elaborate look and have become proficient at mitered cuts. Install the same type of trim in all the rooms before you move on to the next type.

It is easier to get all the painting done before you attach the trim. Once the trim is in position, all you have to do is fill the nail holes and touch up the paint.

Your goal should be to span from corner to corner with a single piece of trim, so cut efficiently. Scrap pieces can be used around columns, or in nooks and bays that can be spanned by shorter lengths.

When turning an outside corner, you should cut miters. For inside corners, use miters or coped joints, depending on the type of wood.

Ceiling Trim

As the name implies, this trim is used to cover the joint between the ceiling and the walls. In contemporary construction ceiling trim is mainly ornamental, although it can be used to hide flaws or disguise imperfections. The simplest ceiling trim is flat, or plain. The most elegant ceiling trim is crown molding, installed alone or with other trim pieces. See illustration on page 101, left.

If you are using flat ceiling trim with board paneling, it is easier to install the trim first, then butt the paneling against it. Any resulting gaps can be covered with baseboard. If you are using trim (crown molding, for example) with an irregular, rather than a flat, back, remember to place the stock in the miter box or against the fence in the same position as that in which it will rest against the wall. Remember too when you make the cut that the mark represents the inside length.

Installing Flat Trim

Start by preparing a plan view sketch of the room to be trimmed. Then decide in what sequence each piece of trim will be installed. Arrange the cuts so that the joints are out of the direct line of sight as you enter the room. If the walls are longer than the stock pieces, use 45-degree mitered cuts to join them. The following installation sequence describes the room shown in the illustration on page 101, right.

Install the trim at the longest wall first, using square cuts at each end (No. 1 on the diagram). Make the piece $1/16$ inch longer than the measurement between the end walls. Hold the piece away from the wall in the center with each end in place and let it snap into position. Now, holding the piece firmly against the wall and ceiling, nail it through the wallcovering into the plates along the top edge and to the studs along the bottom edge. Nail along the entire length of the

piece at 16 inches on center. The nails should be long enough to penetrate into the backing by at least one half their length.

The trim piece at No. 2 on the diagram is next. Cut, fit, and nail it exactly the same as you did the first piece.

Moving clockwise to No. 3 on the diagram, make a coped cut on the appropriate end of a piece of trim stock, test it against the installed piece, and adjust as necessary. The opposite end of this piece is an outside miter; hold the piece in place and mark where it intersects the corner. Check the angle of the corner before cutting the miter. If the angle is either greater or less than 90 degrees, bisect it and cut the miter accordingly. Set this piece aside.

Take a piece of stock for installation at No. 4 on the diagram and cope and fit the appropriate end to piece No. 1. Position the piece and mark for the outside mitered cut. Make the cut $1/16$ inch longer than the mark. With piece No. 3 repositioned and nailed securely in place, hold piece No. 4 in position and check the fit. It should be too tight to fit properly, so cut it (with a power miter saw) or plane it (with a block or Surform® plane) just a little and check it again. If the miter fits well, nail the piece in place. If the miter does not quite fit, shave off a little more until it does.

Now move to the opposite wall (No. 5 on the diagram). Make a coped cut on one end of this piece of trim (to fit against No. 1 on the diagram) and a

square cut on the opposite end. The cut piece should be about $1/16$ inch longer than the measurement. You should be able to hold the piece in approximate position, so that it curves slightly out from the wall, and snap it into place to check the fit of the coped end. Fasten a temporary shim on the wall behind the trim piece to grasp if you have to pull out the trim for adjustments. Adjust the trim as necessary, remove the shim, reposition the trim, and nail it in place.

Prepare piece No. 6 by measuring the distance between wall No. 2 and wall No. 5. Cope both ends of the piece; again, it should be $1/16$ inch longer than the measurement. Position the piece (it should curve out slightly from the wall) and check for fit on both ends. Adjust as necessary, reposition, and nail.

If the last wall (No. 6) is longer than the longest piece of stock, you will have to construct a joint. The best place to put it is over the door, where it will be least visible. A joint requires a bevel-cut at a 45-degree angle. Cope one end of each piece, fit them to their respective mating pieces, cut a bevel with an open face on the longest piece, and nail the piece in place. Measure the distance from wall No. 5 to the bottom edge of the bevel on the long piece, add $1/32$ inch for adjustment, and cut a bevel. Check for fit. Cut or plane as necessary to get a tight fit at the bevel and nail in place.

Glue all the joints and wipe the excess glue off the surface of the trim with a damp cloth. Then set all the nails and fill the nail holes.

Installing Crown Molding

Crown molding is a wide, thin trim that projects out from the junction of the ceiling and walls; it comes in various widths and angles. Because this trim is expensive, take special care in measuring and cutting it to avoid making mistakes. Crown molding does not lie flat against either the ceiling or the wall; rather, it spans the angle between them. Therefore you must provide backing wherever fastening is necessary. You can install backing before or after the wallcovering is applied.

To prepare for installation, and to ensure that the molding is applied correctly, make a template with a scrap of the molding. Hold it in position and with a pencil lightly mark where its edges meet the ceiling and wall.

Don't worry about placing joint cuts out of the direct line of sight; the profile of crown molding makes it too difficult to fit complex cuts at both ends. For crown molding, then, outside corners should be cut and installed first; each piece has a square cut at the opposite end from the miter. You may have to install a long piece with a coped end cut that is more visible than you would like, but the tradeoff in difficulty, and perhaps in wasted material, will be worth it.

Nail crown molding through the flats (near the edges) into the back (see illustration on page 101, left). It is also a good idea to nail outside miters after they have been installed; predrill the holes.

Paneled Wainscoting With Chair Rail

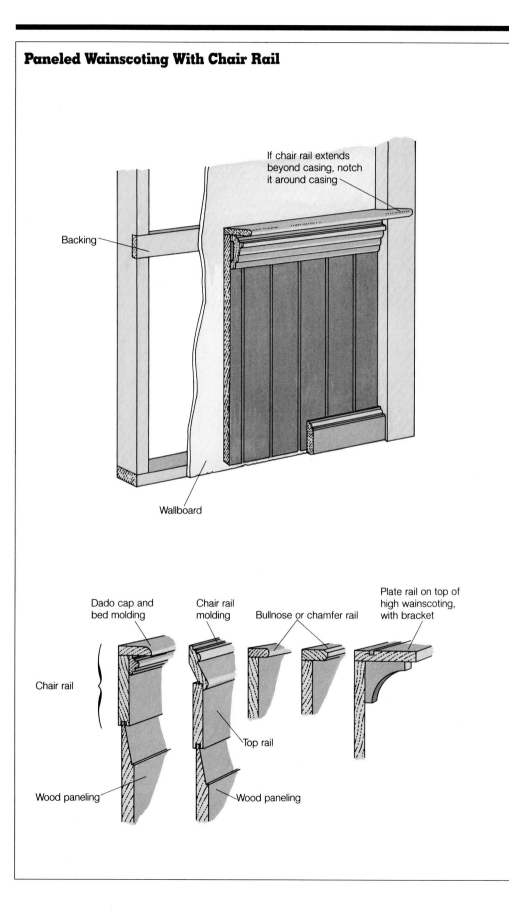

If chair rail extends beyond casing, notch it around casing

Backing

Wallboard

Dado cap and bed molding

Chair rail molding

Bullnose or chamfer rail

Plate rail on top of high wainscoting, with bracket

Chair rail

Top rail

Wood paneling

Wood paneling

Picture Rail

This old-fashioned but clever trim element deserves to be revived. Traditionally pictures were suspended from the rail by hooks and rods or wire; these were unsightly, which may be why picture rail lost its appeal. Today you can use practically invisible monofilament fishing line and spray-paint the hooks to match the trim color.

Picture rail is generally positioned 6 to 12 inches down from the ceiling. Since it is intended to carry considerable weight, you must nail or screw it securely into the studs.

To install the picture rail, snap chalk lines on the walls at the desired distance down from the ceiling. The bottom edge of the rail will be on this line and will cover it after installation. As with the other types of horizontal trim, prepare a plan view sketch of the room and determine the sequence for installing each piece. Miter outside corners and cope or miter inside corners.

Nail into the studs, using the same plan view sketch and installation sequence as described on pages 101 and 102 for ceiling trim. Since the outside miters may project some distance out from the wall, nail them in place. Glue all joints and wipe them clean with a damp cloth.

Chair Rail

Also known as cap molding, this trim was originally installed in dining rooms or other rooms where chairs were moved about, to protect the walls from being scraped. Position the molding according to the height of the chairs that you intend to use in the room.

Chair rail is usually installed about one third of the way between the floor and ceiling, although if you use it as a cap for wainscoting or wallpaper, you may adjust the height accordingly. Follow the same procedure as for other horizontal trim. Plan the installation sequence. Miter and cope the corners. Nail to the studs, following the rules for baseboard. Glue all joints and wipe them clean with a damp cloth.

Chair rail is also used as a border for wainscoting (see illustration on page 103). The molding is grooved on the backside to accommodate the thickness of the paneling. Nowadays many people use chair rail as a purely decorative detail, to divide a wall that is painted at the top and wallpapered at the bottom, or vice versa.

Baseboard

This trim is usually installed last, so that it can be joined to the casings and the wainscoting. It is preferable to install it after a wood finish floor is laid. If this is not possible, the baseboard will have to be elevated with scraps of the flooring to give the necessary clearance. Baseboard is invariably installed before carpeting is laid.

It's a good idea to prefinish baseboard before you install it. Use stain or a clear finish on hardwood and at least a prime coat of paint on softwood. Filling and touching up or final painting can be done later.

The joinery depends on the type of baseboard you use. Flat

baseboard with no decorative profile can simply be butted at the corners. Molded base will have to be coped or mitered at inside corners and mitered at outside corners. A coped inside corner is superior to a miter, because it is less likely to open up after it is nailed.

Baseboard trim can be made up of from one to three separate pieces. See illustration, opposite page. Ideally, the baseboard should not be thicker than any door casing to which it butts up. If it is thicker, butt it up to the point where it meets the casing and then cut remaining thickness back at a 45-degree angle. If you are installing a base shoe along the bottom edge of the baseboard, nail the baseboard to the wall ¼ inch from the top edge. Nail it again ½ inch above the finish floor, position the base shoe over the joint (allowing a ⅛-inch expansion gap between the base shoe and the floor), and attach the base shoe only to the baseboard. This allows the floor to expand and contract without pushing and pulling the trim.

As with any horizontal, or running, trim, prepare a plan view sketch of the room and determine the installation sequence. Arrange the cuts so that the joints are out of the direct line of sight as you enter the room, as with flat ceiling trim. Following the sequence shown above, install the first piece of trim on the longest wall opposite the door (No. 1 on the diagram), using square cuts at each end. Move progressively around the room as you did with ceiling trim. The No. 2 piece on the diagram has one coped cut and one square cut, and the No. 3 piece has one

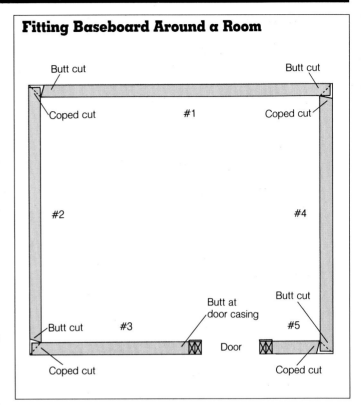

Fitting Baseboard Around a Room

Butt cut · Butt cut · Coped cut · #1 · Coped cut · #2 · #4 · Butt at door casing · Butt cut · Butt cut · #3 · #5 · Coped cut · Door · Coped cut

coped cut and a square cut at the door casing. (If the casing is not plumb, cut the trim piece a little long and scribe it to fit.) The No. 4 piece has one coped cut and one square cut, and the No. 5 piece is cut like No. 3.

When working with outside corners, it is helpful to use scraps of baseboard to mark the intersection lines on the floor, to determine the angle of cut on the miter. After coping or mitering one end of the baseboard and fitting it snugly to the inside corner, mark the baseboard on top at the outside corner of the wall and on the bottom at the intersection lines on the floor. With a combination square draw a vertical line up the face of the baseboard to the top edge. Connect this line across the top at an angle to the mark at the back edge of the

piece. Cut to this line and set the piece aside. Prepare the mating piece using the same method, but make the cut about ¹⁄₁₆ inch longer than the intersection mark on the bottom of the piece. Install and nail the first piece; then fit this second piece, making adjustment cuts as necessary. Install it and nail it in place.

When using baseboard made up of more than one piece of trim, make coped and square cuts in appropriate locations on the cap or on the shoe, or both, for appearance's sake. (Flat baseboard is mitered only at outside corners; inside corners are square cut.) Nail the cap or the shoe or both to the baseboard, in order to minimize gaps caused by shrinkage or expansion.

It is advisable to glue all joints. Make sure to wipe excess glue off all trim surfaces with a damp cloth after installation.

Installing Baseboard

Measuring for Baseboard

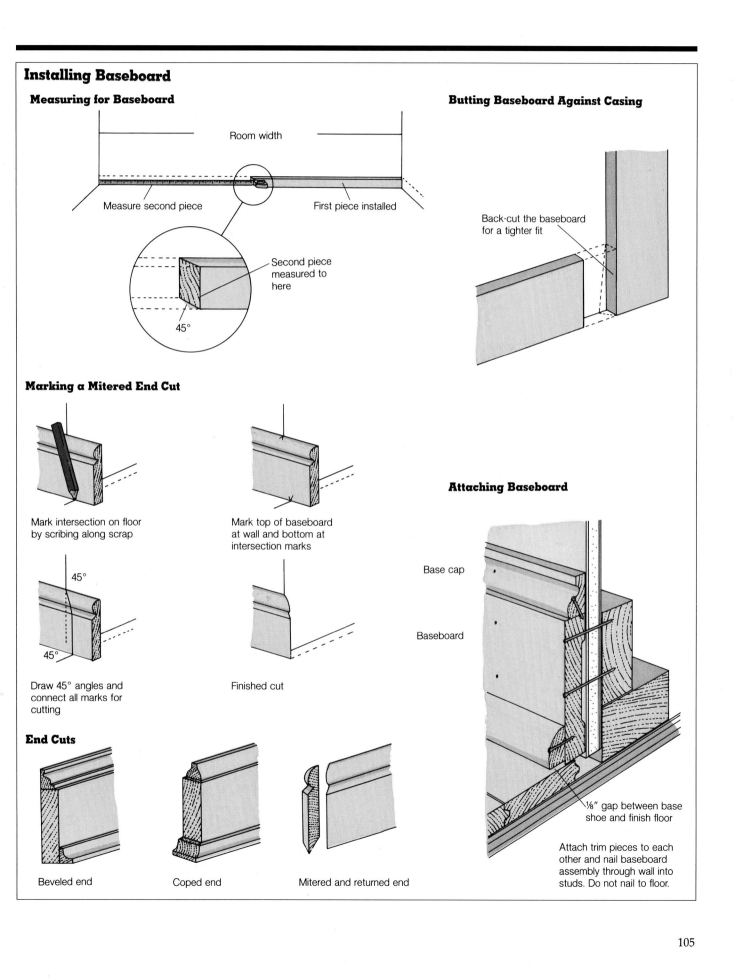

Room width

Measure second piece

First piece installed

Second piece measured to here

45°

Butting Baseboard Against Casing

Back-cut the baseboard for a tighter fit

Marking a Mitered End Cut

Mark intersection on floor by scribing along scrap

Mark top of baseboard at wall and bottom at intersection marks

45°

45°

Draw 45° angles and connect all marks for cutting

Finished cut

Attaching Baseboard

Base cap

Baseboard

⅛″ gap between base shoe and finish floor

Attach trim pieces to each other and nail baseboard assembly through wall into studs. Do not nail to floor.

End Cuts

Beveled end

Coped end

Mitered and returned end

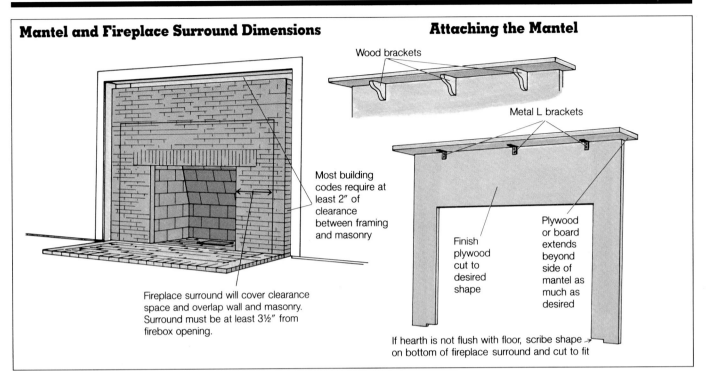

Mantel and Fireplace Surround Dimensions

Most building codes require at least 2" of clearance between framing and masonry

Fireplace surround will cover clearance space and overlap wall and masonry. Surround must be at least 3½" from firebox opening.

Attaching the Mantel

Wood brackets

Metal L brackets

Finish plywood cut to desired shape

Plywood or board extends beyond side of mantel as much as desired

If hearth is not flush with floor, scribe shape on bottom of fireplace surround and cut to fit

Fireplace Mantel and Surround

A fireplace surround is basically an elaborate piece of trim that functions as a casing. It covers the gap between the finish wall and the edge of the firebox in the same way as a door or window casing covers the gap between the wall and the frame. A mantel is a shelf that tops the surround. See illustration, opposite page.

Rather than building a surround and mantel, consider buying a unit ready-made. You can probably order one in the size and style of your choice. To find a local source, check the yellow pages or ask your building-supply dealer. Salvage yards and antique stores often carry old surrounds and mantels that have been rescued from demolished houses.

Caution: Building codes are strict about the setbacks required for flammable materials. Generally any wood trim should be at least 3½ inches from a firebox opening. Any projection, such as a mantel or a hearth, should be at least 12 inches from this opening. Check the local building code for the exact requirements in your area.

Building and Installing a Mantel and Surround

Making your own mantel and surround will be a test of your finish carpentry skills. Because this trim is generally the focal point of a room, all materials, cuts, and finishing techniques will be on display. To ensure good results make certain that miters are perfect and that each piece is carefully smoothed and fitted. For more information, refer to the second chapter.

1. Measure the opening and draw a set of plans to scale. Most surrounds are constructed on a backer board so that the entire assembly can be done in a workshop. Choose a veneered plywood for this piece, since the parts not covered by molding will show. Remember to allow for the thickness of the plywood in your plans.

2. Choose a clear, straight board for the mantel and attach a piece of half-round molding to the front and side edges. Alternatively, cut a design with a shaper or a shaper attachment. Fasten the mantel to the backer board with metal L brackets or wood brackets. If you use metal brackets, cover them with crown molding. See illustration.

3. Attach the trim to the backer board. For the tightest fit start underneath the mantel and work down toward the floor, cutting miters on each piece of trim that turns a corner. Glue each piece and hold it in place with finishing nails. Make sure that these nails penetrate well into, but not beyond, the backer board. Cut the final pieces of molding long and trim them flush with the edges after they are mounted.

4. Carefully fill and sand the outside edges of the surround and mantel (or add more trim after they are attached to the wall). Set all nail heads and fill them with an appropriate putty. Stain or paint the entire surround and mantel. When they are dry, attach them securely in position. Set or countersink the fasteners and touch up the finish.

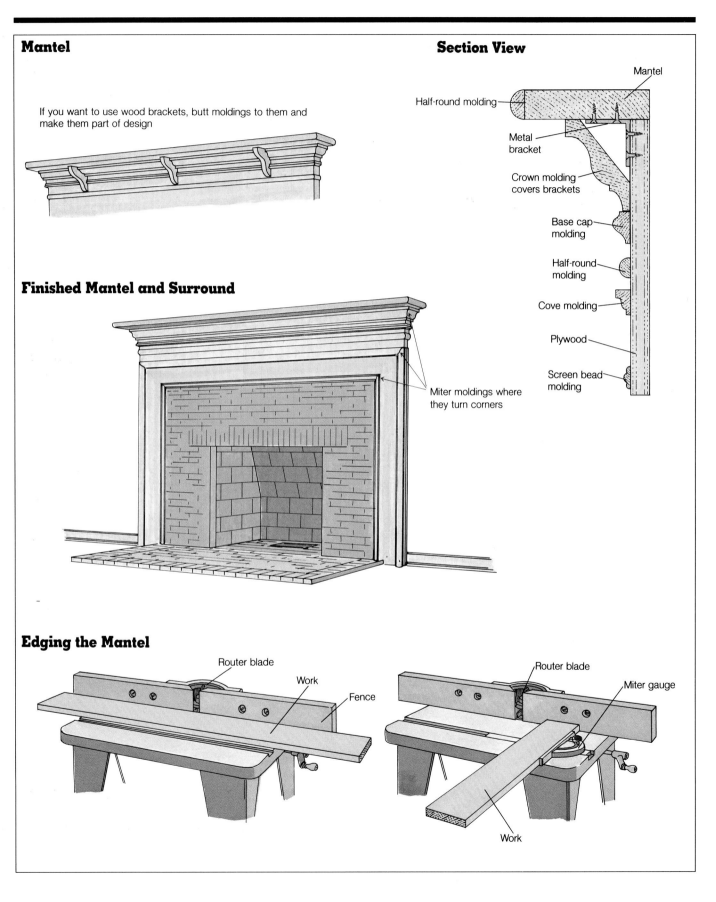

Mantel

If you want to use wood brackets, butt moldings to them and make them part of design

Section View

Mantel

Half-round molding

Metal bracket

Crown molding covers brackets

Base cap molding

Half-round molding

Cove molding

Plywood

Screen bead molding

Finished Mantel and Surround

Miter moldings where they turn corners

Edging the Mantel

Router blade

Work

Fence

Router blade

Miter gauge

Work

Using Standard Trim for Decorative Effects

Installing standard trim pieces against wallboard or wood-paneled ceilings and walls allows you to create various decorative effects. See page 66 for construction details for crisscrossed-beam ceilings.

Top: Trim applied to columns gives stairway a stately elegance. Bottom: Large beams trimmed with moldings (see also page 66) add drama to a living room ceiling.

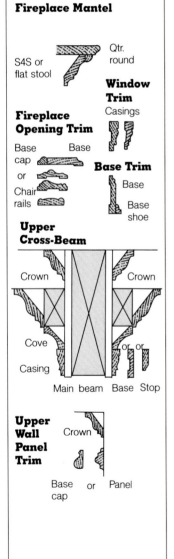

Fireplace Mantel

S4S or flat stool

Qtr. round

Fireplace Opening Trim

Base cap

or

Chair rails

Window Trim

Casings

Base Trim

Base

Base shoe

Upper Cross-Beam

Crown   Crown

Cove

Casing

Main beam   Base   Stop

or   or

Upper Wall Panel Trim

Crown

Base   or   Panel
cap

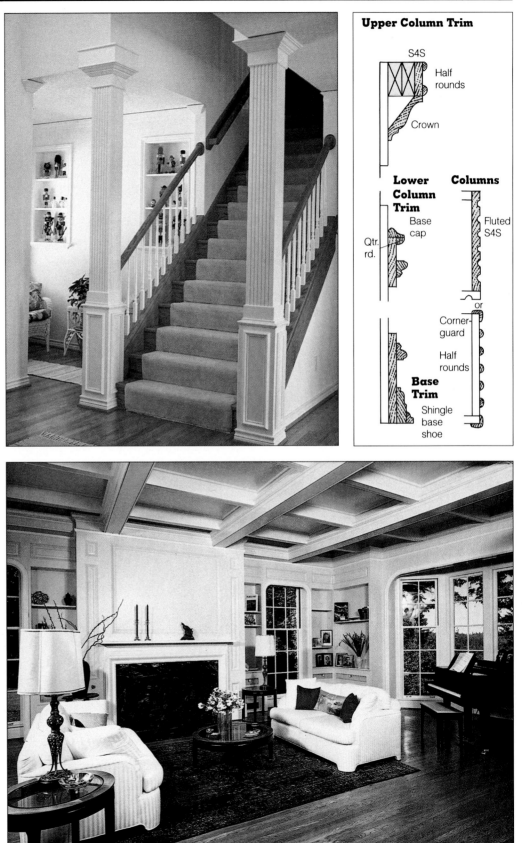

Upper Column Trim

S4S

Half rounds

Crown

Lower Column Trim

Base cap

Qtr. rd.

Columns

Fluted S4S

or

Corner-guard

Half rounds

Base Trim

Shingle base shoe

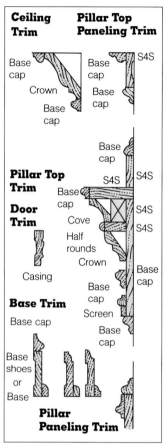

Ceiling Trim

Pillar Top Paneling Trim

Base cap

Crown

Base cap

Base cap

Base cap

S4S

Pillar Top Trim

Door Trim

Casing

Base Trim

Base cap

Base shoes or Base

Base cap

S4S

Cove

Half rounds

Crown

Base cap

Screen

Base cap

Base cap

S4S

S4S

S4S

Base cap

Pillar Paneling Trim

Top: Molding trim provides ornate detail to entryway pillars.
Bottom: Wall panels trimmed with moldings and matching ceiling beams (see also page 66) can lend grace to any room.

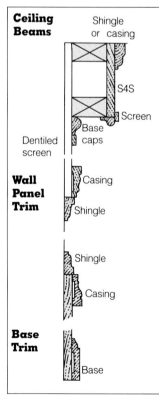

Ceiling Beams

Shingle or casing

S4S

Screen

Base caps

Dentiled screen

Wall Panel Trim

Casing

Shingle

Shingle

Casing

Base Trim

Base

INDEX

Proof-of-Purchase
0-89721-236-3

U.S./Metric Measure Conversion Chart

		Formulas for Exact Measures			Rounded Measures for Quick Reference		
	Symbol	**When you know:**	**Multiply by:**	**To find:**			
Mass (Weight)	oz	ounces	28.35	grams	1 oz		= 30 g
	lb	pounds	0.45	kilograms	4 oz		= 115 g
	g	grams	0.035	ounces	8 oz		= 225 g
	kg	kilograms	2.2	pounds	16 oz	= 1 lb	= 450 g
					32 oz	= 2 lb	= 900 g
					36 oz	= 2¼ lb	= 1000 g (1 kg)
Volume	tsp	teaspoons	5.0	milliliters	¼ tsp	= 1/24 oz	= 1 ml
	tbsp	tablespoons	15.0	milliliters	½ tsp	= 1/12 oz	= 2 ml
	fl oz	fluid ounces	29.57	milliliters	1 tsp	= 1/6 oz	= 5 ml
	c	cups	0.24	liters	1 tbsp	= ½ oz	= 15 ml
	pt	pints	0.47	liters	1 c	= 8 oz	= 250 ml
	qt	quarts	0.95	liters	2 c (1 pt)	= 16 oz	= 500 ml
	gal	gallons	3.785	liters	4 c (1 qt)	= 32 oz	= 1 liter
	ml	milliliters	0.034	fluid ounces	4 qt (1 gal)	= 128 oz	= 3¾ liter
Length	in.	inches	2.54	centimeters	3/8 in.	= 1 cm	
	ft	feet	30.48	centimeters	1 in.	= 2.5 cm	
	yd	yards	0.9144	meters	2 in.	= 5 cm	
	mi	miles	1.609	kilometers	2½ in.	= 6.5 cm	
	km	kilometers	0.621	miles	12 in. (1 ft)	= 30 cm	
	m	meters	1.094	yards	1 yd	= 90 cm	
	cm	centimeters	0.39	inches	100 ft	= 30 m	
					1 mi	= 1.6 km	
Temperature	° F	Fahrenheit	5/9 (after subtracting 32)	Celsius	32° F	= 0° C	
					68°F	= 20°C	
	° C	Celsius	9/5 (then add 32)	Fahrenheit	212° F	= 100° C	
Area	in.^{2}	square inches	6.452	square centimeters	1 in.^{2}	= 6.5 cm^2	
	ft^2	square feet	929.0	square centimeters	1 ft^2	= 930 cm^2	
	yd^2	square yards	8361.0	square centimeters	1 yd^2	= 8360 cm^2	
	a.	acres	0.4047	hectares	1 a.	= 4050 m^2	